by date shown

working with the
tarot

working with the
tarot

unlock the secrets of your
destiny with the tarot

Sarah Bartlett

 A GODSFIELD BOOK

An Hachette UK Company
www.hachette.co.uk

First published in Great Britain in 2010
by Godsfield Press, a division of
Octopus Publishing Group Ltd
Endeavour House
189 Shaftesbury Avenue
London WC2H 8JY
www.octopusbooks.co.uk

Distributed in the U.S. and Canada by
Octopus Books USA:
c/o Hachette Book Group
237 Park Avenue
New York NY 10017

ISBN 978-1-841-81351-6

A CIP catalogue record for this book is
available from the British Library

Printed and bound in China

10 9 8 7 6 5 4 3 2 1

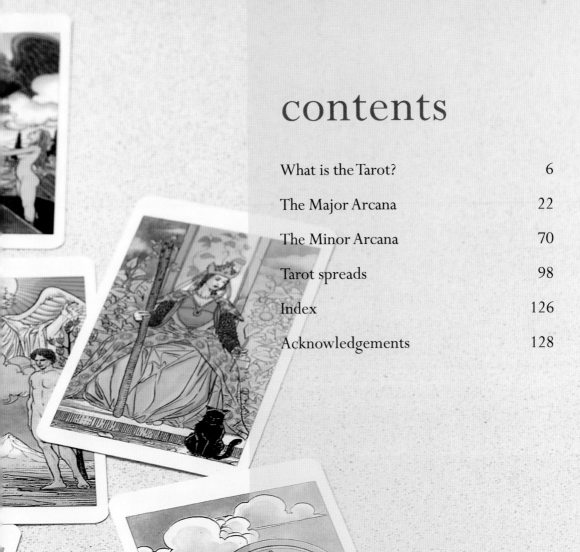

contents

WHAT IS THE TAROT?

The Tarot is a deck of 78 mystical cards that has been used for divination and fortune-telling for thousands of years. It is also used now as a wonderful tool for self-discovery, psychological awareness and spiritual awakening. The Tarot speaks a language that is accessible to all. It is a mirror of the human soul.

the story of the tarot

The Tarot is not only the Fool's journey of self-discovery, but yours too.

The Tarot reveals your potential. It tells you about your hopes or aspirations, and what you project into the future and the outcome of your choices. You can discover the direction you're going in, and what to do about it; how to improve your lifestyle, love life or personal goals and generally develop your own ability to make decisions and the right choice. The Tarot is simply an objective mirror. The great thing about the Tarot is that the cards never lie.

My first Tarot set was given to me by a handsome Egyptian mystic in Paris when I was in my early twenties. I hadn't intended to go to Paris at all, but a friend was driving there in her white Mini, and wanted a companion – so I thought, 'why not?'. That moment's decision changed my whole life. I fell in love with the Egyptian and simultaneously began my first adventure into the world of Tarot.

At first I didn't really know how to interpret the cards, but by drawing one card for the day each day, I began to realize that my life was curiously reflected in the imagery. I began to treat the Tarot as a mirror of who I was and was becoming. Later, I did Tarot readings for friends and strangers alike. My confidence increased and I'd act the part of the local fortune-teller at village fetes where palms were crossed with silver for the local charity. Uncannily, I would always hit on some issue or need that was relevant for the querent (the person asking the question) at that moment, and I began to realize that the Tarot wasn't just a reflection of myself, but was a reflection of the universe at any one moment of time.

The seemingly random choosing of the cards was, in fact, the synchronicity of life itself as we tapped into the energy of the moment together. All that I was doing was interpreting that moment and its relationship to the querent or myself. Now you can too.

In this book, I've created some simple but enlightening exercises that will make it easy for you to understand the archetypal or universal meaning behind the Major Arcana cards (see pages 22–69) and how to interpret them. It will also allow you access to the archetypal nature of yourself. Apart from some fun-to-do visualization techniques I've included simple yoga poses, meditations, creative writing and psychological activities to stimulate your connection to the Tarot. The spreads section (see pages 98–125) also provide you with detailed example interpretations to help you use the layouts and create your own spreads too.

By learning how to work with the Tarot you will also learn the truth about yourself as you go on your own journey of discovery. The Tarot cards are like stepping stones, and just like the Fool, the unnumbered card (see pages 26–27), we may not always get where we planned to go, but it's often by taking a path we hadn't intended to go down that we arrive somewhere that is vitalizing or life-changing, just like my chance visit to Paris.

By choosing one card for the day you can begin to see how the Tarot reflects your life.

tarot history

In the courts of the Middle Ages, the Tarot was used as a card game and for fortune-telling.

The Tarot has been one of the most important Western mystical pathways for hundreds of years. With connections to alchemy, astrology, Kabbalah, Christian mysticism, numerology and many other esoteric traditions, the Tarot is available to everyone.

origins

Nobody is really sure where the Tarot originated, but throughout the last three hundred years or so, historians, occultists and writers have put forth a range of ideas coloured by their own personal view of the Tarot.

Decks of mystical numbered cards existed in India and the East and were probably brought back by Knight Templars during and after the crusades in the Holy Land. There have also been suggestions that travelling gypsies from Egypt brought the Tarot to Europe.

middle ages

Most sources believe that the first Tarot decks appeared in the early 14th century, arising from a combination of early Italian playing cards and the set of 22 Major Arcana, whose origin still remains shrouded in mystery. In the Middle Ages the Tarot was also used to play a game called *tarocchi*, later known as 'Trumps'; still played in Europe today. The earliest cards were hand-painted and one of the earliest decks is the Visconti Sforza tarocchi (*c*.1440) painted for the Duke of Milan.

developments in the 18th century

The French occultist and linguist Antoine Court de Gebelin researched the mystical significance of the Tarot during the 18th century. He claimed the Major Arcana was originally an ancient Egyptian set of tablets of mystical wisdom, remnants of the mysterious Book of Thoth.

Gebelin was convinced these tablets were brought into Europe and hidden by travelling magi (priests who followed the ancient Persian religion of Zoroastrianism) during the medieval period. Gebelin developed his own Tarot deck using 77 cards plus the Fool to make 78. The Major Arcana contained three times seven cards plus the Fool and each of the four suits of the Minor Arcana contained twice seven cards. This became the foundation for most decks ever since, and defined the mystical nature of the number seven.

occultism and the 19th century

During the 19th century, the French Kabbalist and philosopher Eliphas Levi (1810–1875) suggested that the Tarot was rooted in the sacred Enochian alphabet of the Hebrews. In elitist circles, the intellectual occultists believed that the Tarot revealed powerful esoteric knowledge. By the end of the 19th century, Dr Arthur Edward Waite designed his own radical deck with the help of artist, Pamela Colman Smith. Waite was an initiate of one of the most secret groups called the Hermetic Order of the Golden Dawn. The Universal deck used in this book is based on the original Rider-Waite deck as it is now known.

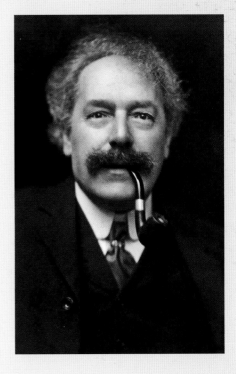

Dr Arthur Edward Waite created the Tarot deck known today as the original Rider-Waite deck.

the 20th century

Later on, in the 1940s, British occultist Aleister Crowley designed the 'Thoth' deck. The controversial magus was notorious for his heroin addiction, and the use of sexual and erotic magic in his own cultish Order of the Silver Star. However, Crowley believed the Tarot was an intelligence in itself and a key to the archetypal world within oneself. This was a turning point for the development of its more recent archetypal and psychological interpretation.

Since then hundreds of decks have been designed, and the Tarot has become more than just a fortune-telling tool; it is a voyage of self-discovery, a mysterious and ancient symbol of all that we are.

how the tarot works

Shuffling the Tarot cards at random is like tapping into the flow of universal energy.

The Tarot works in two ways: first as a symbolic language relying on imagery, numbers, association and a mirroring effect of your personal current situation; and second as a vehicle to tap into the universal energy of the moment.

what is divination?

For thousands of years different cultures have tried to 'divine' the future. Astrologers use the pattern of the planets or stars; palm-readers check the lines on your hand, the *I Ching* is used in the East, and even the patterns of tea leaves have been used to foresee the future. We use the Tarot to see the truth of the moment and thus gain the ability to divine what might also be the consequence of that moment in the future.

engaging with the universe

When you shuffle and draw the cards randomly you're engaging with the energy of the universe. Many people have a problem with the concepts of 'fate' and 'free will'. The Tarot is both – there is choice (free will) and chance (fate) in every moment you are using the cards. This is you.

Drawing a Tarot card is a random thing on one level. Yet is it? Could it be that the card, or rather the flow of universal energy that you are a part of is choosing you? Over time we seem to have lost the awareness that there is a connection between all things in the universe. An invisible energy permeates all, and whether we call it the divine in everything or 'ch'i', this ancient belief sees the patterns of the heavens or the tea-leaves in a cup or another person's life as part of this invisible connection. The Tarot and our apparent random choice of card is part of this process too.

synchronicity

Carl Jung, the great twentieth-century Swiss psychologist coined the word 'synchronicity' to describe meaningful coincidences. He believed that the Tarot card we select unconsciously is generated by something inner that needs to be expressed, or must manifest in the outer world at the moment. We are simply tapping into the universal unconscious.

mirrors

Perhaps the analogy of a 'mirror' is the simplest way to understand how you 'read' the Tarot. Simply, when you draw cards at random, you are drawing little mirrors of yourself. You are reading you. When you look in a mirror do you see what you want to see rather than who you really are? Is your reflection coloured by your perception of what you want to see? The Tarot is a mirror too, and your projections about love, fear, life, dreams and desires are cast onto the cards as they are on the looking glass. These projections are thrown back at you in a symbolic language that you will learn to understand.

symbols

The Tarot is a language of symbols that trigger profound feelings within us and connect to timeless themes and collective dreams. This magic is within all of us, and when we enter the world of Tarot, we enter the symbolic world. Is it just a divination tool for making choices or a learning curve of self-discovery? The answer is both. We eventually learn to read the Tarot as if we are reading our diary. The language of the Tarot is rich in symbolism, and with practice you'll soon know intuitively what the card means to you without having to look it up.

free association

Think about the word 'flower'. Is it a rose, a pansy, a daisy? Do the petals fall, is it just in bud or full bloom, what colour is it? Is it in a garden, in a vase? Once you start working with word associations, they can lead you off at tangents that bring you new ideas, so the original 'flower' can become 'a fading white lily in a jug on the table', not just a flower. This is how you will work with the symbolism of the Tarot, too.

There are many forms of divination developed from different cultures, including palm-reading.

The Order of the Golden Dawn was an occultist cult founded by, among others, Arthur Edward Waite.

the tarot, fortune-telling and psychology

The Tarot has long been associated with the fortune-telling booth at the local fair or fete. 'Fortune-telling' is a popular term for divination these days, but in some ways it has debased the whole art of Tarot.

Back in the late 19th century, elitist occultists who belonged to the Order of the Golden Dawn, considered themselves to be divining the future, whereas the local gypsies were simply telling fortunes. It was easy then for the Tarot to became associated with charlatan 'fortune-tellers' conning ignorant people. Because of its esoteric connections the Tarot was treated with much fear and considered to be as dangerous an art as black magic. Even today there is still much stigma and fear around the Tarot.

Over the past hundred years, however, the Tarot has made a fantastic revival, as an art form, for divination and for popularized fortune-telling methods, but most important of all it is now seen as a very useful tool in the search for self-discovery and psychological awareness.

tarot and psychology

Archetypes are the basis of symbolic divination systems. Jung defined the word archetype as meaning universal pyschic forces or patterns of behaviour which operate in the depths of the human psyche. They manifest in myths, symbols, rituals and instincts, but are hidden within the unconscious; like our instinct for survival, for example, the 'flight or fight' mechanism. We can't see our 'instincts' any more than we can see these archetypal energies at work, but they are there. And we won't have much control over the more primitive archetypes unless we are more aware of the dark and the light within each of us.

Gypsy fortune-tellers are as much 'archetypal' figures in our culture as the Hero or Scapegoat.

These archetypes change and evolve depending on cultural differences and needs of the time, as well as the stages we are at in our lives. But they are essentially those we all recognize, such as the Hero, Heroine, the Lover, the Saviour, the Victim, the Wise Man, the Father, the Mother, the Traveller, the Trader, the Communicator, the Trickster, the Clown, the Achiever, the Scapegoat, the Persecutor, and so on. Then there are the archetypes of 'envy', 'wealth', creativity', and so on. In fact our 'fortune-teller' is as much an archetype in the collective unconscious as is the sorceress or magician. Ironically, the fortune-tellers clichéd phrases such as 'you're about to meet a tall, dark stranger' are valid. After all, who is a tall, dark stranger in the West, but the archetypal hero of our dreams?

As Jung observed, we project onto the Tarot exactly who we are, and by confronting this archetypal world we can begin to free ourselves from our own compulsions and complexes and discover the joy of being part of the universal tapestry of life. As a prelude to beginning to work with the Tarot, take another look at the archetypes listed above. If you could identify with any of the above archetypes right now who would you currently be? Then take a look at the Major Arcana cards and see if you recognize yourself or any of the above characters in the cards.

before you begin

Journals are an excellent way to keep track of your thoughts as you work through the Tarot exercises.

There are a few things to do before you launch into the Tarot, first of which is to scan the structure of the deck and to begin to keep a Tarot journal.

tarot journal

Always keep a Tarot journal. It is useful to make notes on your observations and feelings, and how you worked with the set exercises. If you come up with any new interpretations, jot these down too.

the deck and its structure

The Tarot is made up of 22 Major Arcana cards, plus four suits of 14 cards called the Minor Arcana. This makes 78 cards in all – quite a lot to learn. It is a good idea to start by using the 22 Major Arcana cards on their own. These are very potent symbols and are easier to get to know, and once you feel confident about interpreting the Major Arcana you can move on to the Minor Arcana.

In this book, there is a complete workout for understanding the principles of the Major Arcana. Starting with the Fool, work through all 22 cards using the practical exercises for each card.

the major arcana

The 22 Major Arcana of the Tarot deck represent the most profound and yet the most simple of symbols. The word 'arcana' means 'secrets' while an 'arca' was a deep chest or box. The interpretations given for each card will give you lots to go on, your own interpretations matter too. Flip through the cards now. Look at each card in turn and decide first whether you like it, hate it or feel indifferent. Jot down notes about those thoughts or feelings in your journal, and then read about the meanings of the cards and see which are relevant to you now. Each Tarot card has keywords and key phrases for quick interpretation.

The 22 Major Arcana are numbered 1 to 21, plus The Fool, which has no number, but is sometimes referred to as 0.

the minor arcana

The Minor Arcana consists of 56 cards in four suits (Swords, Wands, Pentacles and Cups) from ace to ten, which are similar to a normal card deck; plus four court cards (rather than three) of the Page, Knight, Queen and King. Begin to use these once you are familiar with the meanings of the Major Arcana. The Minor Arcana has more to do with the events, people and experiences you encounter in life. These cards are just as important as the Major Arcana but don't have the same in-depth energy.

spreads and card positions

Throughout the interpretations of the cards I refer to 'you now', 'blockage', 'the past', 'the future' and 'outcome' positions. In the example spreads there will sometimes be a card within a spread that represents the past, one that represents the future,

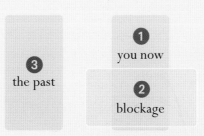
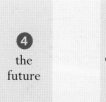

and one that 'blocks' the 'you now' card. 'Future' cards are usually placed to the right of the layout, 'past' cards to the left. The 'you now' position is usually the first card to be drawn, and the 'blockage' card placed horizontally crossing it. 'Outcome' cards are usually the focal point of the layout and are often the last cards to be drawn. Look at the diagram for an example of all these positions in a layout.

reversed cards

A reversed card occurs when you draw a card or lay it out and the picture is upside-down facing you. Most Tarot readers consider reversed cards to mean the quality or energy of that card is lacking or not available to the querent in some way. If you are a beginner, don't worry about reversed meanings nor think of them as negative. Turn the cards the right way up; upright cards will reveal just as much as you need to know.

getting started

Before you can start, you will need to choose a deck that suits you, learn how to care for it, as well as take on board tips on how to set the scene, shuffle and draw cards before you begin to read for yourself and for others.

choosing and caring for your deck

Nowadays there are many special Tarot packs associated with everything from fairies to rock 'n' roll. Opt for one of the traditional packs such as the Rider-Waite or Universal decks where the pictorial images are easier to understand. When caring for your deck, there are no rules, but treat them well. When you first take them out of their box lay them out on a clean table, and allow them to 'breathe', both exuding their energy and taking in yours. Connect with them. Touch them, pick them up, study them. Take your time, and once used, either return them to their box, or wrap a silk scarf around them to protect them from harmful sunlight or inauspicious energy.

Make sure the environment is calm and undisturbed so you can get in a relaxed, intuitive frame of mind.

set the scene

Always read Tarot cards in a quiet place. Focus clearly on what you want to know, light candles, burn incense or just have gentle soothing music in the background to enhance the atmosphere. Don't try to do too many readings in one day about the same issue; it will only confuse you.

As long as we don't deny responsibility for our future choices, the Tarot reveals uncannily past, present and future patterns of behaviour. When you first start practising with a card for the day, you'll see how the card corresponds to the energy, experiences and events over the following 24 hours.

shuffling

There are no rules to shuffling. It's simply a way to make the choice of card as 'random' as possible. While you're shuffling, concentrate on the issue or question you have in mind. If you can't shuffle them like a deck of playing cards in your hands, spread them out face down on a table and swirl them around in a circle until you feel intuitively the cards are ready to be drawn together into a pile. You can also cut the cards a few times afterwards. If any cards are reversed, then turn them upright when you turn them over. I always use the cards the right way up because all values, whether good, bad or indifferent, can be found in the upright card.

drawing the cards

Place the pack face down and then shift them gradually to the left or right until you have made a long line of overlapping cards. Keep thinking and focusing on your question or issue all the time. Then when you're ready, slowly run your finger along the cards. Stop when you feel a card seems to ask to be picked. You can close your eyes to do this while focusing on your question or issue.

You can run your fingers across the spread out cards until you sense the right one to pick.

reading for yourself and others

Always try to be objective when reading for yourself. It's very easy to see what you want to see when reading for yourself, but the cards never lie, only people! So look up the interpretations and work with the ideas in relation to your issue/question.

If you do opt to read for other people, establish that your 'querent' has either a specific question he or she wants answered or just guidance and advice. Always take as much care reading for others as you would yourself. It's easy to see what you think the person wants to hear or project on to the cards your own current issues, rather than be totally objective. That's why good practising on yourself before working with others is really important in developing this level of reading.

daily-card, one-card and open-card readings

You can benefit from getting to know all the cards by choosing a daily card. Every morning pick one card to see what kind of day you can expect, what kind of tasks you might need to perform, or who is going to come into your life.

Beforehand, write down in your journal what you think will be relevant to that day. Later on decide what the card referred to. Did it have meaning and relevance in a different way or the way you interpreted initially?

one-card answer

If you want to consult the cards to confirm your feelings or instincts about a situation or decision you can simply draw one card without doing a layout. Look up the interpretation and relate it to your problem.

interpretation skills

The hardest part is not looking up interpretations in the book! Of course when you're beginning it's probably the surest way, but as you improve you must learn to develop your intuitive skills, working with both your intuition and the traditional symbolic meanings in tandem.

I learned to interpret on my own by using a free association technique. Simply look at the imagery of one card – say the Magician. What is he doing? What colours stand out? What do Magicians mean in your life? On the table he has objects representing each of the suits. What does this imply? Could this man be active, engaged in sorting out the world. His wand is pointing to Heaven and the other hand to Earth. Is he trying to ground something? And most importantly, tell a tale to yourself about each card aloud. When we start expressing our train of thought, we can achieve amazing breakthroughs.

what do I ask?

The easiest way to start with the Tarot is by asking specific questions. Once you've familiarized yourself with the cards, you can do what is called an 'open reading' and see what turns up (see below). Start out with just one, two or three cards. The simplest questions reveal the best answers. Don't try and twist your question because the Tarot doesn't judge, only you do. So you might have a relationship question. Try not to ask negative questions or ones that confuse the response.

Loaded questions
• When will my job situation improve?
• Should I go to France or Italy?

Instead rephrase
• I intend changing my job; can you give me some idea of what would be suitable for me?
• I want to go to France; is this a good time?

Always write your questions down in your journal before shuffling, then you can't cheat!

Tell yourself a short story about the Magician to help you focus on what the card symbolizes.

open readings

Sometimes you might just want to get a general sense of what's going on in your life. This is where open readings come in useful. When you shuffle and draw the cards, try to relax and be open to the energy, without thinking consciously of anything. There is usually an underlying motive for open readings, but they can be very useful for finding out what theme or problem needs expression. Keep a note in your journal of the reading and whether it is a theme that crops up frequently in your life.

Finally, most of the spreads in this book are aimed at personal self-development. Questions aren't asked, but what happens is they raise questions in yourself about who you are and what you really want.

THE MAJOR ARCANA

The Major Arcana, meaning 'great or big secrets', represents the most fundamental energies in life. These 22 cards are rich in imagery in all tarot decks, regardless of which set you choose: some bear the figure of a person (or several people in some cases); some represent scenarios, and all are loaded with many symbolic images. Some cards will leap out at you and you'll have an immediate connection with them. Others, you just won't like and some will provoke no reaction in you at all.

what is the major arcana?

People often feel uneasy about the Devil, but it has positive meanings as well as negative ones.

The Major Arcana symbolizes our most basic issues at a universal level. The cards to which you react most strongly are highly reflective of your own current needs and issues.

If you fear 'the Devil' for example, meditate on that card and work with its meaning and archetypal energy within yourself. If you can avoid projecting positive or negative values on to the cards, their rich symbolism will generate self-honesty. As you work with each card try to take an objective view of yourself and what the card says to you.

Spread them out across the table or floor in their numerical order. The Fool at zero is placed first, followed by the Magician at one, and so on. Let your finger move across each card and if any gives you the shivers or you feel a rapport with the card, look up the basic interpretation. This is your very first spread and will give you a sense of the mirroring effects of the Tarot.

exercises

Learning to interpret these cards isn't difficult, if you practise the specific exercise designed for each card. I suggest you start with the Fool and follow in chronological order the Tarot journey I have set out in the following pages. If, however, you feel you understand the symbolism and meaning of a card, you can always leave it out. But by actually engaging in the experience of the card, you learn how this energy is present in you, too. Even if you've done some Tarot work before, this is a totally new and enriching approach to experiencing the Tarot.

I have included a range of exercises such as guided imagery, yoga poses, imaginative techniques, creative activities, chakra work and even a mood board to take you deeper into the world of Tarot. It's a magical journey of discovery. It will free you from the assumption that the card is separate from you. It's not only a mirror of who you are, it is you. You are the Tarot.

the fool the magician the high priestess the empress the emperor the hierophant

the lovers the chariot strength the hermit the wheel of fortune justice

the hanged man death temperance the devil the tower the star

the moon the sun judgement the world

the fool

The Fool is the child within who is about to journey forth without a care in the world, not knowing about the hardships and problems we all have to face in life.

symbols and meaning

The Fool usually implies new beginnings and an enthusiasm for life or a personal quest. The Fool is smarter than you think. Even though it appears as if he was about to walk off the edge of the cliff, could there actually be another ledge a pace away from him on to which he might step? Only he knows if it is an illusion or not. This card reminds us that sometimes resistance is more 'foolish' than risk.

In relationship questions, watch out that you're not falling in love with love or that you are being blind to the truth about where a relationship is heading. The Fool can mean that you won't listen to anyone's advice and that you are being careless with feelings. You may be blind to future heartaches or rushing into a new venture too soon without thinking things through.

position interpretations

ZERO OR UNNUMBERED

Astrological affinity Uranus
Keywords Impulse, infatuation •
Blind to the truth • Child-like •
Pure and uncorrupt, spontaneous
• Adventurous • Eternal optimist •
Ready for a quest

In the 'you now' position, the Fool signifies you're ready to move on or to take a leap of faith; in the 'blockage' position, this card can imply you have an immature or irresponsible attitude towards everything that is preventing you from moving on. In a 'past' position, it's likely you were too naive to accept a situation, and in a 'future' position you're about to go on a journey of self-discovery or fall in love too fast.

reversed meaning

Spontaneity is lacking in your life, or you feel you haven't the energy to achieve anything.

setting out on a journey

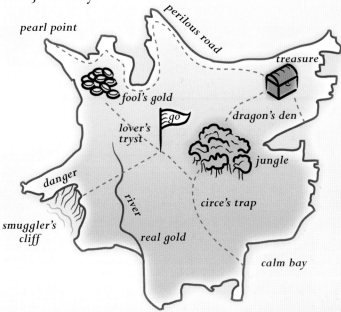

The Fool represents our spirit of adventure and also the way we set out on our journey to find ourselves. By creating your own hidden treasure map, you will see how the Tarot itself is a journey of discovery. You are going to start out on your own Tarot journey by first getting to know about the Fool.

You will need Paper, pen, imagination
You will feel Excited, challenged, innocent
Result Know that the Fool represents your inner child

1 Like the example map on this page, draw yourself a huge island shape of your choice.

2 Put a marker or box of hidden treasure at some random point. Then make paths across the island. Draw in some signposts or magic places. For example, I've marked 'Fool's Gold', ' Real Gold', 'Smuggler's Cliff, 'Circe's Trap' and 'Dragon's Den'. It doesn't matter how many you include, or really what you call them; what is important is that you are investing your own spirit of child-like adventure into your own treasure hunt. This is the purpose and interpretative sense of the Fool. By creating your 'treasure island' you can then embark on this Tarot journey with the excitement of knowing that you're eventually going to find the treasure chest, the 'arca' or secret box of self-awareness, and a deeper connection to the Universe.

3 Once you have finished drawing your map, imagine yourself setting off to this island for a very big adventure. Then carefully roll it up and tie with a ribbon or string. Place it in a safe place. You're not going to look at it again until the end of your journey.

the magician

The Magician is the archetypal miracle-worker. Knowing that he has the power of the Universe behind him, he puts ideas into action. Everything he does is with full knowledge of his own motivations.

symbols and meaning

The magician reaches one hand up to the sky and the symbolic world, the other to the ground and the material world. When imagination, ideas and reality merge we create magical results and a sense of achievement. When you draw this card as a daily card, for example, it's time to juggle with ideas, adapt to changing circumstances, and find the appropriate way to act.

The Magician also represents masculine creative energy and the potency of male sexuality. In business affairs it can represent your ability to turn the tables in your favour or resolve a situation that no one else could.

position interpretations

If the Magician appears in the 'you now' position, you're flexible, active and ready to achieve a goal. In the 'blockage' position, the Magician can indicate that you're so focused on your goals, you are ignoring your values. In a 'future' or 'outcome' position, you'll either have to manifest your dreams or guide a friend or partner towards making the right choice for themselves. In a 'past' position, you've set the pace and inspired others, which has led to a sense of achievement.

ARCANUM ONE

Astrological affinity Mercury
Keywords Initiative, persuasion, action, concentration, focusing on a goal • Acting with awareness • Getting magical results • Wisdom the key to success • Don't deceive yourself that you know all the answers

reversed meaning

You haven't yet acknowledged your true intentions or you don't have any goals you think are of any value.

visualizing your inner magician

This exercise to get to know the archetypal Magician uses a visualization technique about manifesting your dreams.

You will need Chair or bed, imaginary wand
You will feel Focused, self-aware
Result Understand how the Magician in you creates magical results

1 Sit or lie down somewhere peaceful and quiet, where you won't be disturbed by the telephone or other people. Begin to relax by concentrating on your breathing.

2 Close your eyes and create a mental picture of a huge bubble above your head filled with the colour red – the colour of initiative, purpose and desire.

3 With one hand reach up like the Magician and pierce the bubble with your finger or imaginary wand. As you do so imagine the red slowly flowing through your finger into your hand, and through your body until you are filled with red. Now imagine you feel full of desire, invincible and infallible.

4 Gradually let the colour red wash slowly back up through your body towards your fingertip so the red flows back into the bubble.

5 Next create a mental picture that you're connected to the Earth, and that your feet are roots reaching down into the Earth's crust. Now imagine that deep within the ground the colour green permeates the world's interior – the colour of manifestation.

6 Next imagine the green slowly moving up through your feet, legs, torso, arms and head until you are completely green. Imagine you're ready for action.

7 Gradually let the green subside back down into the Earth. Let go of both red and green in your mind.

8 Now open your eyes and write down in your journal what it is you truly desire and how you're going to act upon that desire.

the high priestess

ARCANUM TWO

Astrological affinity Mercury
Keywords Secrets, hidden
feelings, intuition • The healer,
feminine power • Silent potential •
Mystical influences • A secret will
be revealed • Seeing beyond
what's obvious • Trusting in your
inner guide • Being receptive

The High Priestess is a passive, feminine card. It is the archetype of all that is unknown, mysterious and unconscious.

symbols and meaning

On the Fool's journey, his meeting with the Magician was his first encounter with the power of the material world. Now, his encounter with the High Priestess lets him know that there are other less worldly forces at work in our lives. We must go within to acknowledge our unlived potential, which remains in the shadows. Unless we attempt to work with the dark side of ourselves, we won't see the true light. When you draw this as a daily card it's timely to accept that there is mystery in life, just as there is factual knowledge. This card also symbolizes feminine power and the mystical nature of femininity or the lunar qualities of life.

position interpretations

In the 'you now' position, the High Priestess often indicates there are secret desires in your heart. Perhaps you are finding it hard to communicate your feelings? In the 'blockage' position, this card can indicate you fear finding out how you really feel about someone. Develop your awareness and use your intuition about what you really want and where you are going. As an 'outcome' card you will soon be enlightened about a problem, or a secret will be revealed. As a 'past' card, think back to what someone said to you recently; it may give you an answer to a problem or enlighten you as to why you feel uneasy.

reversed meaning

In the reversed position this mean that you are not trusting your inner voice or are repressing your talents.

finding your hidden self

Try this mirror exercise to get in touch with the High Priestess and to enable you to interpret this esoteric card more easily.

You will need Mirror, candle, favourite crystal, chair
You will feel Aware of your hidden power
Result You realize how the High Priestess symbolizes the hidden side of yourself – the beginning of self-knowledge

1 At night place your favourite crystal and perfumed candle on a shelf or ledge in front of a mirror. Light the candle and lean the card of the High Priestess against the mirror and look at the card. She is seated in front of an embroidered veil that hangs between two pillars. Beyond the veil is your unconscious, beyond the veil is the mysterious other.

2 Next hold your crystal in your writing hand and offer it palm up and open to the High Priestess. Think of one secret you would never tell anyone, and tell it to the High Priestess out loud or in a whisper if you think someone might overhear you.

3 Place the crystal back on the ledge and look at yourself in the eye in the mirror. See the High Priestess in you? Again, pick up the crystal and offer it now to your reflection and this time tell yourself the one secret you would never tell anyone.

4 Now you have told both the High Priestess and your reflection the only secret you would never give away. How do you feel? Relieved? Disconcerted? Whatever you feel, feel it, whatever you see in the mirror in your eyes or in the High Priestess, let yourself see it. Open your mind to all that you feel, see or experience and then replace the crystal on the ledge.

5 Close your eyes and say this affirmation: 'My hidden potential is there before me, I only have to look.' Now open your eyes and see this mirrored before you.

the empress

ARCANUM THREE

Astrological affinity Venus
Keywords Abundance, female
vitality • Sensual pleasure,
nurturing • Feeling good about life
• Connecting to nature •
Mothering others • Creative and
material reward

The Empress represents the earthly pleasures of the world, and the creative and fertile aspects of the feminine spirit.

symbol and meaning

This is the ultimate 'Earth Mother' archetype, generous and giving. When you draw this card as a daily card, you can be assured of progress in any plan, however daunting it may seem. Or that your mothering or sensual skills will come to the fore in some way. It also implies that if you want to become a mother or act in a motherly way, this is a great time for conception of offspring of both the body and mind. The Empress emphasizes your need to stay grounded, to not lose touch with the natural rhythms of life and the sensuality of the world around you. This symbol encourages you to embrace the worldly as well as the intellectual or spiritual.

position interpretations

In the 'you now' position, the Empress indicates you might have to motivate your partner or mother them! As a 'blockage' card, it can suggest there is a disruptive female influence in your life or that your own mothering instincts are getting in the way of true love. Motherly love can be 'smotherly' love too. As a 'future' card, material wealth or property will be successful for you in the future, but it's also time to be creative with your life rather than assume things will just fall into your lap. The Empress reveals that you must feel as well as think your way through life.

reversed meaning

If the Empress is reversed you have no trust in your instincts or you feel sensually inadequate in some way.

getting in touch with your creative feminine side

To enable you to interpret and connect to the Empress archetype more easily, this exercise asks you to delight in abundance.

You will need Pen, nature, journal
You will feel At one with nature, sensual and creative
Result You understand how the Empress symbolizes the creative, sensual action of the feminine

1 Find a beach, park, mountain, field, anywhere you can get 'back to nature', even your own garden if you have one, where it is peaceful and you can be alone.

2 Then do any or all of these things: feel the grass beneath your bare feet; touch the leaves of plants or trees; smell the lavender, roses, the damp earth or the newly mown grass; watch the sunset; gaze at the wide open sea; listen to the birds; hear the surf wash along a shore; smile at a sparrow; feel the wind in your hair, the rain on your skin, the sun on your back. Experience the sensual world of nature in all its abundance.

3 When you have really and truly felt 'at one' with Mother Earth, write down in your journal the following and add your own endings:

- I take pleasure in …
- I adore …
- Mother Earth to me means …
- I enjoy …
- I am grateful for …
- Warm feelings come to me when …
- I feel joy when …

Notice how the world of the Empress has touched you.

the emperor

In order to balance the lavish, self-indulgent nature of the Empress, the Emperor represents the masculine principle of order and structure. The Fool has encountered the power of the archetypal Mother, now he must meet the archetypal Father.

symbols and meaning

This card is all about structure, laws, leadership and authority. When you draw this as a daily card it suggests it's time to organize your life, be rational, forward-thinking and tie up any loose ends. You're in an ambitious phase and can make headway with any of your plans. The Emperor can also indicate that you're about to encounter an authority or father-figure, or that some legal or official matter needs attention. This card can also signify that you will fall for a 'father-figure' type in a relationship question.

position interpretations

As a 'you now' card it's time to take control of the situation and face the facts. As a 'future' card it can mean you will be attracted to a strong dominating person or a successful career go-getter. Gold-diggers and cold-hearted lovers are also signified. They may seem reliable in bed or around the office but could be simply on a power trip. As a 'blockage' card, someone in power is stopping you from achieving your aims, or you fear going against the expectations of your own father or someone who has a strong hold over you.

reversed meaning

If the Emperor is reversed, there may be a lack of order, or you feel chaotic. You can't structure your ideas nor do you have a clear vision of what you want from life.

ARCANUM FOUR

Astrological affinity Aries
Keywords Power, authority, father-figure • Leadership • Power of reason • Insensitivity to others' feelings or desires • Assertiveness • Taking control • Getting organized • Working within a system • Establishing law and order

---

feel the power

To open up to the power of the Father archetype and to enable you to work more immediately with the Emperor, use the simple yoga Tadasana (or mountain) pose to feel the strength and power of your spine, symbolic of the 'back-bone' of the Emperor's rule.

You will need Just you, barefoot, in loose-fitting clothes
You will feel Vertical – 'I'm walking tall'
Result Knowing that you are as majestic as a mountain and your inner authority exists

1 Stand up straight with your feet close together. Close your eyes, arms by your side and concentrate your mind down into the soles of your feet. Rock a little forwards into your toes, then back into your heels until you feel a place of balance.

2 Feel the weight of your upper body spread evenly through your feet. Feel yourself rooted to the floor. Now open your eyes and gaze ahead.

3 Bring your mind into the base of your spine. Pull back your front thighs slightly opening up the area between top of legs and trunk of body. Draw the abdomen in and tuck in the tailbone slightly to bring the buttocks into line.

4 Lift the chest up and away from the abdomen; keep your buttocks in and lengthen the spine upwards to the crown of your head.

5 Soften your shoulders, and let them drop away from your ears as the top of the chest opens up. Lengthen the back of the neck, relax the throat and bring your attention to the uprightness of your back and spine.

6 Press down through your feet and notice the flow of energy moving upwards through your spine. Stay here for a moment or two. Be aware of the vertical calm and strength of yourself, the Emperor.

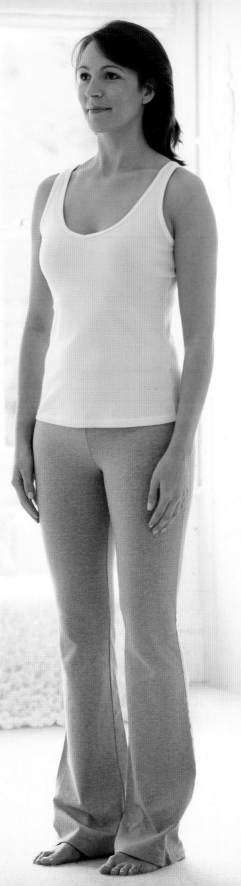

the hierophant

ARCANUM FIVE

Astrological affinity Taurus
Keywords Conformity, education, holding back • Respect, teaching • Traditional rules and ceremony • Doing what's expected of you • Devoting your time to a belief system • Pursuing knowledge

The word 'Hierophant' is rooted in ancient Greek and means 'an expounder of sacred mysteries'. As with most knowledge we have to learn it from someone, whether a teacher, guru, spiritual teacher or just through the university of life.

symbols and meaning

The Hierophant is the archetypal mentor and represents all these roles. He may be a religious figure, part of the Establishment, or a team leader, but he is concerned with rules, belief systems and rituals. When you draw the Hierophant as a daily card, it can indicate you'll need to conform to the group, or that important or secret knowledge will be imparted to you.

position interpretations

If you draw the Hierophant in the 'you now' position, you may be stuck in your ways and are unwilling to adapt to others. Clinging to traditional principles means that you can't move on and accept the necessary changes that will improve your life. In a 'future' position, the Hierophant often represents a specific person who you will meet, someone who has good advice, or a guru, adviser or teacher who should be trusted. It also implies meeting someone you feel you've known before and with whom you have a rapport. If you draw this card as a 'blockage' card, you may be fighting against a restrictive influence such as an orthodox group of people or dogmatic friend or counsellor who seem to stop you from trusting your own belief system.

reversed meaning

If you draw this card reversed it may indicate that you don't know where to put your faith.

the glade of knowledge

Try this guided imagery technique to access the archetypal Hierophant within you.

You will need Imagination, journal
You will feel Like a guru
Result You understand that the teacher lies within you as without

1　Relax in a quiet place where you won't be disturbed, either sitting or lying down.

2　Close your eyes and imagine you are walking down a country lane towards a glade of trees. The sun is high, there are large cumulus clouds in the sky and it is late spring. Birds sing, wild flowers dance in the breeze and ahead of you the wood is filled with glistening colours from new leaves and blossom that glint in the sun.

3　As you reach the glade you see a tree that stands out from all the others. Its roots tangle across the ground towards a small stream that meanders away from you. Its trunk is gnarled and twisted, ancient and battered by the ravages of time. Its branches are wild and overgrown, bursting with new life, each leaf sparkles silver.

4　Beneath this magical tree is a circle of stones, each inscribed with sacred words, unreadable mystical signs and glyphs. Imagine that you sit within the centre of this stone circle and close your eyes.

5　You reach out to take up one stone and as you hold it in your hand you open your eyes and read mystical words inscribed on the stone, which say: 'I now know where to put my belief, it is in myself'. Stay in this circle for awhile; when you're ready to leave, place the stone back in its place.

6　Now write the stone's affirmation in your journal along with the sentence: 'I am healing myself through sacred knowledge written down for me.'

the lovers

ARCANUM SIX

Astrological affinity Gemini
Keywords Love, choice,
temptation, commitment • Power
of love and how we deal with it •
What do you mean by the word
'love'? • Physical attraction •
Making a decision • Knowing
what is right for you • Sexual
harmony • A love triangle

So far you've met five different 'people' on your Tarot journey. The Fool, or 'you' now comes face to face with love. How do you deal with it?

symbols and meaning

What does love mean to you personally? Did you mark a 'Lover's Tryst' on your treasure map (see pages 26–27) or was it meaningless in your quest for the hidden treasure? Whatever the case, you now have to meet 'love' whether in its wildest, most beautiful or even painful forms. This is a card that we all want to draw in a spread, but like any other card it has both positive and negative values depending on our personal projection of good and bad qualities and the circumstances of the reading. Love is a word that can mean commitment and conditions to some, or it can mean freedom and no conditions for others. The Lovers archetype is also about the urge for sexual union and our quest for eternal love. The Lovers card also asks you to question the values and opinions of others or whether your own values are truly yours.

position interpretations

In the 'you now' position you want to fall in love, get closer to someone or commit yourself. If single, you may simply be looking for romance; attached, you may be feeling good about your partner and yourself. But there is still something missing or new romance could come into your life without you even looking for it. This card also implies it's time to make a relationship choice. Do you commit? Will your partner commit? Do you go your separate ways?

Conflicts can be resolved if this card is in the 'future' position, but can also indicate that temptation will test the strength of a current relationship. Love triangles are also indicated by this card in a 'future' position, or that you will have to choose between two people.

In the 'blockage' position, the Lovers suggests you're blinded by love or refuse to take responsibility for your choices. You may be involved in a love triangle or a third party could be indicated. The Lovers can also imply you need to find out what your true values are, and if you have a decision to make, it would be appropriate to know exactly what you believe in before taking action. Someone may be urging you to do one thing when you'd rather do something else. Dare you go your own way?

reversed meaning

If you draw this card in the reverse postion, it indicates low self-esteem or a 'how could anyone possibly ever love me?' attitude.

journal work

Because this card is easy to remember and its influences are widespread, I've included more possible interpretations than with other cards. Rather than a specific exercise, it would be more appropriate for you to simply write down exactly what 'love' means to you. It can be one word or a novel's worth, that's up to you. Or ask yourself what you want from a relationship really? Of course, these thoughts or feelings will change, so keep your mind open and work with this card as a meditation tool as often as you can.

But one thing you must do is write the following line in your journal: 'The Fool, in his quest for union, learns that it takes two to take one out of oneself.'

the chariot

ARCANUM SEVEN

Astrological affinity Cancer
Keywords Diligence, will-power,
honesty, perseverance •
Archetypal achiever • Control over
feelings and thoughts • Learning
to stick to the right path • Trusting
in yourself • Being determined •
Asserting your ego • Sexual
prowess • Wanting victory

With self-belief the Charioteer knows he is going to defeat his enemies and conquer new lands. Similarly, the archetypal hero or achiever has no fears and is ready now to persevere for his own purpose.

symbols and meaning

There may be choices to be made, but with conviction and sheer grit, this card is symbolic of all to do with self-assertion and ego. When you draw this as a daily card, you will have the confidence to get what you want or you might meet someone who gets things done their way. This might, of course, conflict with your own way. This card asks you to think about your own ego: how healthy is it; are you wilful; or are you willing to get things done? The Chariot also indicates sexual prowess, so in a relationship question, it can indicate someone who seeks sexual power over you or that you have issues around power.

position interpretations

As a 'you now' card, there may be conflicting influences in your life, but you have now reached a point where you can stand up for your own beliefs and make decisions based on what you want rather than what other people assume is right for you. You can now achieve success in any enterprise and overcome all obstacles in your way. As a 'future' card, timing and control are essential to get what you want, so don't let the reins slip through your fingers; stay on top. Maybe your relationship needs re-evaluating? Whatever your mission, only you can make it work.

reversed meaning

If the Chariot turns up reversed it means you may be feeling defeated or doubting yourself.

have faith in yourself

This exercise will help you have more faith in yourself by affirming your passions and goals.

You will need Scraps of paper, pen
You will feel Elated
Result A reinforcement that the Charioteer's mission is to trust in your identity and have faith in yourself

1 In your own handwriting, write down a list of what makes you feel self-assured and confident about yourself and then make another list of those things that make you wobble like a jelly. Write them on little scraps or separate bits of papers. You can write as little or as much as you like for each category.

- I want …
- I have a passion for …
- My greatest talent is …
- My current goal is …
- I feel confident when …

- I hate …
- I get angry when …
- I don't want …
- My self-esteem is low when I …
- I fear …

2 Think about the reactions and feelings that come to you when you write all this down. Look at the words as you write them, look at them again afterwards.

3 Now put them to one side for a while, then look at the words again a few hours later – they are all powerful symbols of YOU.

4 The Charioteer within you is going to conquer any negative thoughts or feelings, so crumple up the pieces of paper with the negative words on them and throw them all into the bin. Take the positive words and learn that these are the vital life-affirming bits of yourself. Say them every day on waking.

Now the Fool in you has mastered the art of being the Charioteer.

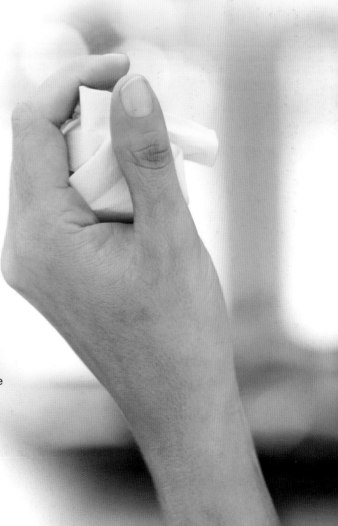

strength

ARCANUM EIGHT

Astrological affinity Leo
Keywords Inner strength,
courage • Self-awareness,
personal power • Facing
reality • Taking responsibility
for your life • Ability to forgive
• Being compassionate •
The strength of love • Being
tolerant

Far away from the Charioteer's battleground and warring 'Look at me!', is the strength that comes from emotional or spiritual self-awareness.

symbols and meaning

The Fool has learned to acknowledge the ego – the Charioteer – to get a mission accomplished, but he must now discover that quiet determination and the power of gentle persuasion can work in his favour, too. When you draw this as a daily card, it's timely to reflect on how self-aware you really are. Do you have compassion for yourself? Can you forgive yourself for your faults as well as others? Can you take responsibility for your decisions, behaviour and actions without feeling guilt or blaming anyone? It also reminds you not to give up or give in, for you now have the inner strength to persevere.

position interpretations

If Strength appears in the 'you now' position, it is time to gently force an issue to achieve results. You have a huge reserve of strength of character, so don't doubt yourself. If you are asking a question concerning love or romance, are you giving too much of yourself or not getting anything back from a partner? In the 'future' position, self-awareness and courage will bring you success. Gentle persuasion or a little passive seduction will help you get closer to someone. As a 'past' card, your compassion has seen you through to better times. As a 'blockage' card, are your kind heart and compassionate nature preventing you from making the changes you truly want?

reversed meaning

If Strength turns up reversed, then you have very little inner strength and need to develop some boundaries.

strengthening the chakras

Many Eastern traditions maintain that energy circulates around the body through energy centres known as chakras, the Sanskrit word for 'wheel'. The state of your chakras reveal your well-being. To be in the best shape, physically, mentally, emotionally and spiritually, your chakras need to be nurtured and any negative energy that 'sits' in the chakras cleansed or unlocked. In this exercise you're going to use the power of your mind to strengthen them. On the accompanying illustration the seven main chakras of the body are indicated, along with a keyword for each colour of chakra energy. While you strengthen your chakras, imagine the corresponding colour filling that chakra with its coloured light (see page 124 for the qualities associated with each chakra).

You will need Your body, the floor
You will feel Cleansed
Result Being compassionate with yourself is the key to Strength

1 Find a calm place where you will be undisturbed and can work alone. Once you are in this relaxed state sit cross-legged on the floor and imagine the strength of your base chakra at the base of your spine, and how it is firmly rooting you to the floor.

2 Holding your hands about 7.5 cm (3 inches) away from your body over this chakra centre, fingers pointing to each other and not quite touching, move them up to the area of the sacral chakra, just below your navel.

3 Meditate on the qualities and colour of this chakra for a minute or so, then move up to the solar plexus chakra; again imagine the colour and quality of this chakra and feel or experience it within. Do the same with the other four chakras, then gently place your hands back down into your lap.

4 Now calmly close each chakra by working down your body starting from your head – imagine that each chakra is protected by a pair of shutters on a huge french window and you are now closing them. Once you have closed all the chakras in order from head to base, smile at yourself for strengthening the inner you. Know that Strength is compassion.

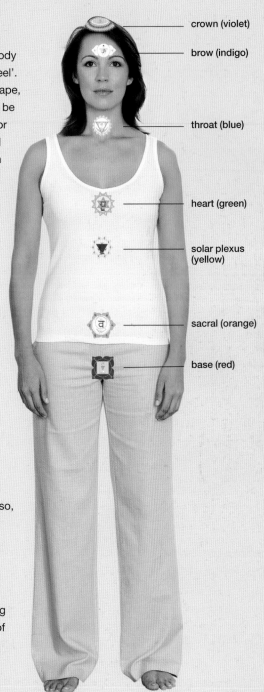

crown (violet)

brow (indigo)

throat (blue)

heart (green)

solar plexus (yellow)

sacral (orange)

base (red)

the hermit

At some point in our lives we stop, put down tools and wonder what it's all about – life that is. This contemplative side of our nature is symbolized by the archetypal Hermit.

symbols and meaning

Each of us is existentially alone – ironically the one thing we all share. The Hermit represents the urge for some solitude, the need to understand the world and to find answers. The Fool discovered compassion and courage within, but now he wants to know some answers about his own quest. Whatever you are looking for when you draw this card it's timely to take a step back and think long and hard before committing yourself. What are your underlying motivations for doing what you do? Ask yourself what you truly want. Soul-searching doesn't have to be a chore; it can be fun, too.

position interpretations

In the 'you now' position reflect carefully before you make a choice and avoid rushing ahead with plans that could push others into doing something against their judgement. If it's a relationship issue, maybe you need time to contemplate or you fear revealing a secret? As a 'past' card you may have chosen to forget certain facts or are refusing to face up to the truth. As a 'future' card you will have to put your plans on hold until you can decide what is right for you. In the 'blockage' position, the Hermit suggests you're trying too hard to find the answer when it's probably staring you in the face.

reversed meaning

If this card turns up reversed, you will find greater comfort in company than being alone right now.

ARCANUM NINE

Astrological affinity Virgo
Keywords Discrimination, discretion, detachment, withdrawal • Developing inner wisdom • Knowledge is a burden • Fear of revealing a secret • Searching for the truth • Wanting solitude • Looking for direction

---

create a mood board

Advertisers and designers use mood boards to create a 'feel' for their range of fashion, TV set or theatre design. They use swatches of colour, fabric, photos cut out of magazines, sketches of their designs and other bits and pieces to create a collage. Create your own mood board around whatever it is you are currently seeking. It might be a job, a talent, a partner, a spiritual belief or an idea for a novel.

You will need Paper, photos, pins, glue, bits and pieces
You will feel Contemplative
Result Knowing that those who seek shall find

1 Gather together all your bits and pieces and images, along with a piece of paper large enough to hold your mood board. You don't have to be an artist, but use either symbolic images of what you seek or photos, material objects, or paint your desires on canvas if you're feeling daring.

2 Put the passion of yourself into the mood of the thing/desire/dream you are seeking.

3 Keep your mood board on your desk, bathroom, stuck up on the fridge, anywhere you pass or sit or visit frequently during the day.

4 Every time you look at your mood board think of the positive qualities of the Hermit and how solitude also brings about great creativity of the mind and the soul. When you created your mood board, hopefully, you were alone. Solitude has its purpose too.

the wheel of fortune

The Wheel of Fortune represents the dilemma of both fate and free will in our lives. Sometimes life seems to come at us in the guise of chance encounters, unexpected events and good or bad luck. Sometimes we take chances and snatch opportunities.

symbols and meaning

When you draw this card, even though you are inextricably linked to the greater cycles of universal energy, it's about taking responsibility for your choices rather than blaming things solely on 'fate'. The Fool has contemplated, he's seen that the choices he's made so far have led him to the present moment. Now he's ready to move on again and has a sense of being part of the whole. The Wheel says, 'Don't feel the world is against you, be part of the cosmic dance and enjoy it.'

position interpretations

In the 'you now' position, a new phase in your life is now beginning whether you want it to or not. Don't fear change, instead embrace it for future happiness. In a relationship issue, the Wheel can signify infatuation or a new romance, escaping from a difficult relationship or improving an existing one. It's time to jump on the bandwagon and take the chances that are coming your way. As a 'future' card, unexpected events will give you the motivation to change your life for the better. As a 'blockage' card, you believe you are fated, that you have no control over your life, but it's the very lack of responsibility for your choices that is creating the problem.

ARCANUM TEN

Astrological affinity Jupiter
Keywords Inevitability, destiny, timing • There is no certainty in life except uncertainty • Each moment is a new beginning • Only constancy is change itself • Seeing cycles repeating in life • A turning point • Movement or coincidence

reversed meaning

If this card turns up in the reversed position, it's not a good time to take chances. Wait until the energy is with you again.

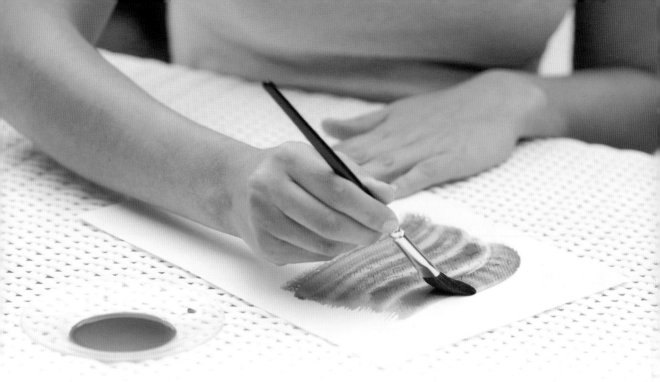

grab opportunities

Many things have been written in sand. I'm sure you've seen the squiggles, signs and words on many a holiday beach. In fact, it's likely that every beach in the world would be covered with words if we listed all the decrees, judgements and condemnations of human failings and achievements and wrote them in the sand. Yet, those beaches are mostly deserted, and tides and time wash the words away.

You will need Sandy beach, big stick, imagination or paper, pen and paint
You will feel Ready for a new adventure
Result Know that the Wheel of Fortune is about taking opportunities rather than fearing them

1 Find a beach, empty, windswept and wild. Carve your wish-list into damp sand in huge bold letters made with your feet or a big stick. If you can't literally get to a beach, then imagine doing this in your mind or write it out on a piece of paper, marked 'My Beach'.

2 Punctuate each wish with exclamation marks and question marks – is this what I really want? Or is this what I have been conditioned to want?

3 Then, when it is all clear to you, when unreal wishes are erased, rewritten and set out like a giant agenda on that lonely beach, wait for the tide to come in. Or in your mind imagine the words vanishing under the surf, the sea dredging them away, washing them clean. If you used paper, paint the sea over your wish-list with large swathes of blue ink or watercolour paint.

What you have done, either symbolically in your head or literally out there in the landscape, is write your own fortune. Things written in the sand have a habit of becoming mighty truths. You have connected to the Wheel.

justice

ARCANUM ELEVEN

Astrological affinity Libra
Keywords Fairness, harmony,
equality • Objective thoughts and
balanced relationships are
favoured • Interaction and
communication are essential now
• Cause and effect • Knowing why
you are in a certain situation •
Making decisions

'Madame Justice' holds the sword of decision-making in one hand and the scales of impartial judgement in the other.

symbols and meaning

This card represents all that is fair in love and war. However, what is fair to one person may not be so to another. When you draw this card you're being asked to take a rational view of the situation and avoid personal feelings. Justice asks us to look logically at ourselves. You should not be judgemental about your actions or someone else's. The Fool has understood how he can create his own fortune, but Madame Justice reminds him that he must also learn to make choices and take responsibility for them and their subsequent outcomes.

position interpretations

In the 'you now' position, you need to make a decision and you'll be able to do so with a more rational viewpoint than before. As a 'past' card it implies you've got what you set in motion and things are going to improve. Whatever the results of a series of events, things will now work out for you. Legal issues are often indicated by this card as a 'future' position and will have a successful outcome. If you're looking for love, it can indicate a charming, diplomatic admirer will come into your life. As a 'blockage' card, Justice signifies that you or someone else is being too compromising and preventing you from moving forwards or making a decision.

reversed meaning

If this card is reversed, it means that you are far from being able to think rationally. In fact, you're better off trusting your instincts than the judgement of others.

be your own judge and jury

Do you consider yourself to be a 'goody-two-shoes' or a devil in disguise? Perhaps neither, just ordinary, but for this exercise you become your own judge and jury.

You will need Just you
You will feel Non-judgemental
Result Ability to see beyond good and bad

1 Start by relaxing somewhere quiet and peaceful where you won't be disturbed. Close your eyes.

2 Think about all the things you did yesterday and place a positive judgement on each action. For example, you went to the post office, stood in line politely and said thank you. You gave a busker some coins – how generous you were. Exaggerate your goodness, become a saint, the most dedicated friend, the most virtuous partner. It doesn't matter if you were truly like this or not, but I want you to really judge yourself as pure and untainted as you possibly can, and then judge your friends or colleagues in this way too.

3 Now change tack. Make your judgements negative. See yesterday's actions and events as wicked. Look for signs of manipulation, spite, revenge and loathing in everything you did yesterday and see yourself as deserving of punishment.

4 Now step out of the role of judge and see yourself yesterday from an objective point of view, neutral, with no invested goodness or badness in you.

You are as fair as Justice herself.

the hanged man

One of the most mysterious cards in the Tarot, the Hanged Man is enigmatic and complex. Remember that the upside down world of the Hanged Man is simply that and you'll get the 'hang' of this card.

symbols and meaning

This card invites you to do exactly the opposite of what you believe is right for you to do to gain results. The Fool now faces hardship in his quest; suddenly all that was true and fair isn't; but by letting go of his high expectations the Fool paradoxically finds he can feel free of pressure. His priorities change and even though his world is turned upside down, he can, like the Hanged Man, see the truth from a different angle.

position interpretations

In a 'you now' position this card means you are at a crossroads and may have to stand back and look carefully at all the issues involved. You're in limbo about what you want to do next or are going through a cease-fire in a relationship clash. The contradictory nature of the Hanged Man also suggests you might need to make a sacrifice rather than have things your way. The Hanged Man also warns you about sacrifices. Relinquishing something is sometimes necessary but think clearly if you are being manipulated by others. As a 'future' card you will undergo a change of mind and an adjustment of your feelings will be necessary to go ahead with your plans. As a 'blockage' card, your reluctance to see your problem from a different angle is what's holding you up.

reversed meaning

If the Hanged Man turns up in a reversed position, do things your way and don't make sacrifices at any cost.

ARCANUM TWELVE

Astrological affinity Neptune
Keywords Transition, limbo, paradox • Sacrifice may be necessary • Bored with life • Anticipation of progress • Static relationship • Taking one step back to leap forward • Changing priorities • Doing the opposite of what is expected

giving yourself a different view

This is a simple but effective yoga position that develops the theme of the Hanged Man in helping you see a situation from a different point of view. It is known as the Downward Facing Dog.

You will need Floor, journal
You will feel Paradoxical
Result You'll see a situation from a different perspective

1 Kneel on all fours on the floor with fingers facing forwards, then 'walk' your hands further forwards with your palms flat on the floor.

2 Raise your trunk, straightening your legs and keeping your feet as flat on the floor as possible. Pull in your abdomen. Your head should relax down in line with your arms and body. The shape of this asana is an inverted V.

3 Hold the pose for as long as is comfortable. Let your thoughts flow and experience a new perspective. Imagine you are the Hanged Man, neither uncomfortable nor cosy, in limbo, yet seeing the truth hidden in its opposite.

4 Come down onto all fours, and then when you are ready, stand up. Record your thoughts, feelings and impressions in your journal.

You have just 'hung out' with the truth of the Hanged Man card.

death

ARCANUM THIRTEEN

Astrological affinity Scorpio
Keywords Change, new
beginnings, transformation •
End of an old cycle and beginning
of a new one • Letting go of the
past • Accepting the inevitable
• Finalizing unfinished business
• Closing one door, opening
another

This card often spooks people, but don't take it literally. This is one card in the Tarot where we project our greatest fears.

symbols and meaning

Death is a positive card in all positions and is an energy concerned with transition and change. Something ends and something else begins. A new cycle is beginning, the old gives way to the new. The Fool now realizes that he must eliminate aspects of himself, both his own habits or negative qualities but also opinions, pointless goals or unnecessary people in his life and move on. We all do this at some point in our lives. We have to drop the old 'me' and develop a new sense of self; put value into a new cycle and let go of the past one. Some of us deal with this well, while others cling to the past and can't move forwards; the card tells you it's time to do so.

position interpretations

Death simply implies that something has reached the end of a cycle. When in the 'you now' position it can imply you are in the process of changing your life but are perhaps concerned about the consequences. In the 'future' position it relates to imminent change, which will bring vitality and a completely new you. In the 'past' position, you've already overcome a transition period but you might not yet have accepted or 'mourned' the loss of the old you. As a 'blockage' card, Death implies you fear change so much it's the fear that is stopping you from achieving your current goal.

reversed meaning

Death in the reversed position may mean that the cycle hasn't reached its natural end yet, and you need to attend to what is, not what will be.

embracing change

Does this card make you feel fearful? Does it suggest bleak, dark mortality in all its forms or can you see through to the truth of this card, that change is something positive and brings movement and opportunity into your life? If you stick to this exercise faithfully, you'll realize how 'change' can be a friend who walks the same pathway and helps you close doors in order to open new ones.

You will need Life
You will feel Purged
Result Understanding that 'Death' is with you every second of the day

1 This exercise is best done literally out there in the big wide world. Make a decision to go somewhere you have never been before. Or to do something one day you have always longed to do but never dared. For example, if you've never been to a health spa or the top of a mountain, decide to go.

2 Observe your initial reaction to even thinking about this. Do you shiver and quake with fear? Do you smile and think 'oohh, that's going to be fantastic'.

3 Now plan your route or book the hotel room; whatever the practicalities, attend to them. Get on the bus, jump in the car. Walk. Whatever your choice and decision you are going there.

4 Just as you approach your intended experience you change your mind. Not in fear or to escape, but simply to experience the 'experience of change' as vividly and as actively as you can. You must now make a sudden decision to go somewhere else. Anywhere as long as you 'change' your mind. Observe how this makes you feel as you go off at a tangent. Do you fear change or leap happily into this risky business of changing your mind?

Change your mind and you change your world. Death embraces this change, it can lead you down a pathway that is life-changing for the better.

temperance

The archetypal angel is in us if we choose to look, but usually we're more concerned with outer events, daily problems and how to deal with the side of ourselves we don't like that much.

symbols and meaning

Temperance is a card that asks you to blend different aspects of your life or mix things in the right proportion and create something positive for yourself. Temperance, as the word suggests, represents the balancing of energies and the knowledge that by adding more information or taking away unnecessary behaviours, we create answers to problems.

position interpretations

Good management of your relationships is in process. There is harmony between your desires and your needs, and you are mentally and emotionally in balance. If you're trying to make a decision, you will find a solution and it will be much easier to see another person's point of view. As a daily card, it's timely to combine ideas, people or resources to create harmony. Think angelic thoughts today, banish all others and welcome the angel's centredness. As a 'you now' card, your self-control and willingness to compromise are a good influence on others. As a 'future' card, you may have to moderate your desires and try to see both sides of an argument. But clarification of your true goals or aspirations is coming your way. As a 'blockage' card, you may be too willing to compromise, and trying to please everyone else is at the root of your problem.

reversed meaning

If Temperance turns up in the reversed position you may have a lack of harmony, too many emotions or feelings over-riding the stillness within.

ARCANUM FOURTEEN

Astrological affinity Sagittarius
Keywords Self-control, compromise, moderation • Virtue • Blending of ideas • Harmony and understanding • Moderation will create balance • Need for cooperation • Healing energy • Being centred • Vitality and well-being

---

restoring harmony and peace

Try the yoga Child pose or *Balasana* to restore harmony and bring about a sense of peace.

You will need Cushion, floor
You will feel Restful and balanced
Result Being in harmony with oneself and the card Temperance

1 Kneel on the cushion and keep your knees together. Sit back and rest your buttocks on your heels.

2 Lengthen your spine, then tip forwards from the pelvis so that your upper body folds over your thighs and rest your forehead gently on the floor. Move your arms backwards towards your toes alongside your thighs with the backs of your palms resting on the floor.

3 Relax your shoulders and let the energy dissipate through your arms, melting away all tensions. Hold this pose for as long as you like and meditate on your inner 'angel' as you begin to feel centred.

4 Return to the sitting up kneeling position and move your knees wide apart. Once again sit back on your heels, then lengthening your spine, lean your the upper body forwards, resting your forehead on the floor. Keep your buttocks in touch with your heels, then stretch forwards with your hands as far as you can on the floor. Relax into the pose for as long as you like and enjoy the sense of awareness that modification of your pose increases harmony ... as does the Temperance of our lives.

the devil

ARCANUM FIFTEEN

Astrological affinity Capricorn
Keywords Illusion, ignorance,
sexual temptation, materialism,
living a lie • Thirst for money
or power • Unconscious
reactions • Child-like responses
• Being obsessed • Allowing
someone to manipulate you •
Limited perception

The word 'devil' comes from the ancient Greek for 'adversary', and it is our own worst enemy – oneself – that springs to mind when we draw the Devil.

symbols and meaning

This is a sign that we are living a lie, fooling ourselves about the truth, believing what we want to believe or being limited in our perception. The Devil can also refer to apparent outer difficulties; temptations, such as money, sex, materialism and the need for power. The Devil basically symbolizes all that is bad, but we can't have bad without good, and it is the mistakes we make about what is good and bad which distorts the truth. As a daily card it asks you to accept your limitations or to be aware of living under other people's expectations.

position interpretations

When this card is in the 'you now' position it can simply mean you are attracted to someone for lust or money. Or you are getting involved in a relationship and are confusing desire with love. As a 'blockage' card, it's likely you're living a lie, or ignorant of what's really going on in a relationship. As a 'future' card, you are going to have to fight against the temptations of materialism or power, or take care you are not led astray by someone who wants to take control over you. Sometimes this card reveals that you are acting like a child, without awareness of your actions or the consequences. When you draw this card frequently, it signifies that you're labelling everything and everyone with negative thoughts. This needs to be flipped to positive energy for yourself.

reversed meaning

If this card is reversed, you're free from a manipulative situation.

attracting positive energy

Try this exercise to regain a sense of positive energy.

You will need Imagination
You will feel Released
Result Discover the gift of emotional honesty

1 Relax somewhere quiet where you won't be disturbed and close your eyes. Imagine walking down a long road, where you've been, what you were doing before and why you are on the road.

2 Cross a beautiful valley and find a huge cave in cliffs to your right where you stop to rest. In the cave is a stone tablet covered in velvet cushions upon which you rest.

3 Imagine you close your eyes. A shaft of pure white light beams down on you from a fissure in the cave empowering you. Imagine the light filling every cell of your body, your mind, your spirit, your feelings, your thoughts – all your energy is being topped up with cosmic energy.

4 Now imagine that energy as any colour you love right now. Visualize the flow of colour around and through you, then still radiating that colour, walk out of the cave.

5 Continue walking down the road where you will meet a stranger who is instantly attracted to you. Imagine what colour that person is radiating; does it clash with yours? Does it match, do you like it or hate it?

6 Holding the colour in your mind, open your eyes. Whatever colour the stranger was radiating is the 'colour' you are currently attracting into your life. If you loved it, then you'll attract positive energy into your life; if you don't like it then you're still putting out negative thoughts and feelings. Be honest.

Don't live the Devil's lie, live the Fool's truth.

the tower

ARCANUM SIXTEEN

Astrological affinity Mars
Keywords Sudden change
• External disruption •
Unexpected events or challenges
• Breakdown of the old to herald
the new • Acceptance that no
defence is totally secure •
Learning to adapt and adjust •
Chaos all around

The Fool has seen the Devil and how bound he was by his own illusions. The only way he can free himself is to learn to adapt quickly to new experiences, to let go of the past and not fear the unexpected.

symbols and meaning

Some people find this card invigorating; chaotic yes, but there is a breakthrough here. A sudden crisis is a way of waking us up to the truth. Unlike the cyclical change of Death, the Tower is surprising, unpredictable change, and you may find this card unsettling if you are someone who attempts to control your life. The Tower's lightning strike reminds us that we can't assume anything, and we also need to shift perspective and not cling to those beliefs or opinions that no longer serve us any purpose. As a daily card, you need to recognize that something has to change.

position interpretations

There is, or is about to be, an unexpected change in an external manner when this card appears in the 'you now' position. It might even seem at the time that 'fate' takes over and that you're not responsible. The Tower in the 'future' position reveals a catalyst or outside influence will come into your life to instigate those changes and you won't be in control. It can feel liberating or uncomfortable, but you now have the necessary strength to adapt and move on. As a 'blockage' card the Tower indicates that you're refusing to see the truth or you're so fearful of the unexpected you won't shift your viewpoint.

reversed meaning

If the Tower turns up in a reversed position, you are so in control of events or so stuck in your ways that not even a crisis will divert you.

ranting and raving to release

This card looks like trouble. So you're going to BE trouble.

You will need An empty, hopefully sound-proof room
or a solitary place outdoors
You will feel Released
Result Ready for anything

1 Find yourself a solitary place where no one can hear you. Start by
saying everything out loud. Say exactly what it is you dislike about
your partner, friend, mother or whoever, then what you hate
about them. Why the government is a total disaster
according to you. Get cross about something that
happened to you recently. Attack a friend's opinion or
an ex for the way they treated you.

2 Feel confident in your anger. Enjoy your
performance. Get raving mad about whatever
it is. Pummel the cushions, stamp your feet,
throw a plate, rage like a toddler. Feel the
anger rise in you, observe your warring
propensity, scream what you hate most
about life, yourself, the world.

3 Keep going and try to observe yourself from
outside yourself and see how all that anger
is a real Tower of Destruction. Get it out of
your system.

4 Now suddenly stop and be surprised at the
stillness. The unexpected change from the
wild to the civilized is as revelatory and as
sudden as the Tower's symbolism. You have
been 'sudden trouble' personified, and now
you are prepared to experience anything.

Like the Fool your dark thoughts have been
blasted away in an instant.

the star

ARCANUM SEVENTEEN

Astrological affinity Aquarius
Keywords Inspiration • Ideal love
• Truth revealed • Realization of a
dream • Insight and self-belief are
essential for happiness • Seeing
the light • Finding peace within •
Feeling generous

We wish on stars and we draw inspiration from the cosmos as we turn away from the Devil of materialism and the Tower's intrusion in our lives.

symbols and meaning

The Fool now realizes that he can experience the unexpected. He's ready to be inspired, to look to the stars and have faith in his future. Similarly, when you draw this card you are assured of the calm after the storm. The Star provides you with your personal light of hope and your powers of self-expression will be at their highest. You feel in touch with universal energy and you're ready to navigate by the stars or your own ideas and truth. The Star is an abstract card and therefore doesn't give you any practical solutions. But if you believe and trust in yourself, you can create your own opportunities.

position interpretations

In the 'you now' position, this card is all about having an optimistic attitude. This card is beneficial in any layout and indicates success in love, work or financial aspiration. As a 'future' card it reveals that a revelation is about to come to you in the nicest possible way. The only downside of this card is when it's in the 'blockage' position and indicates that your expectations are so high that no one, not even yourself, can live up to them. As a 'daily' card, observe how inspired you are by events or people or your own thoughts. Do you think to yourself, 'I'm going to do this because I believe I can?' See the light of who you are during the day and feel at one with yourself.

reversed meaning

The Star in the reversed position means that you feel there is no hope or that you cannot believe in yourself.

wish upon a star

If you are lucky you can literally wish upon a star for this exercise, but only if you have access to a cloudless night sky, no light pollution and some form of 'lying on your back' arrangement. If not, then simply imagine the stars above.

You will need Stars in the sky or your imagination
You will feel Inspirational
Result Knowing that the Star is always there to guide you

1 Relax as usual. If you are lucky enough to be able to lie directly under the stars don't close your eyes; if you're using your imagination, close your eyes.

2 Begin to see or look for stars. To start you will only see the brightest, but as your eyes adjust to the dark, imaginary or otherwise, you begin to see more distant twinkling lights. The planets will stand out, and depending on which hemisphere you are in, certain constellations will appear.

3 Imagine yourself up there in space beside the stars. They're your companions, you're another star, just next to that one there. Think big, think BIGGER, how big can you think? Is infinity possible? How do you measure 'bigness' when all around you is space?

4 Then take one star or planet into your mind and make a wish. Believe in that wish and that star as your guide. Now you will feel blessed, hopefully you will feel elated, inspired, a visionary with a mission. But whatever you feel, feel it. Stay looking at the night sky a little longer, in awe and in wonder at which star is yours and yours alone.

You have just had an encounter with the infinite nature of yourself.

the moon

ARCANUM EIGHTEEN

Astrological affinity Pisces
Keywords Fear, self-deceit,
warning, illusion • Tricky love affair
• Blind to the truth • Unrealistic
dreams • Feeling lost • Worried
and apprehensive • Trust your
instincts/intuition

The Moon is deceptive. It is a warning about losing yourself in worries, vulnerabilities or illusions, but at its best it enables you to plunder the depths of your unconscious and let the shadows come out to play.

symbols and meaning

When the Fool first confronts the Moon he has just been inspired by the Star, but now he's beset by so many thoughts and feelings, he is bewildered. When you feel 'lost' it's hard to know where to turn. When we are overcome by fear, either from the darker shadows of our own mind or feeling apprehensive about making a decision, this is the Moon's territory. Mystery permeates life and the shadowy side of ourselves needs expression at times. When we come face to face with the Shadow of ourselves, we feel vulnerable or unrealistic. We must learn to trust our intuition.

position interpretations

As a 'you now' card this may be a warning that things are not all they seem. Maybe you are wrong, your judgement unsound or someone is taking advantage of you. Try to tap into your intuition rather than your imagination. As a 'future' card someone will be dishonest; either you or a partner or friend. It also indicates that you're so wrapped up in your emotions that you don't have a clear rational view of the truth of a matter. As a 'blockage' card the Moon suggests its your insecurity that holds you back or that your sense of not belonging to anything, not even yourself, is the root of your current situation.

reversed meaning

If the Moon turns up in a reversed position, don't rely on your intuition right now; better to use logic to sort out any issues.

accessing the dark side

This exercise will help you understand that the Moon reflects both your fears and your imagination.

You will need Small pouch or paper bag, pebbles or runes, paper, journal
You will feel In touch with your intuition
Result The dark side of the Moon is accessible and not so scary

1 Write a list of all the things you currently fear – irrational phobias, losing your partner, having no money, being unloved, saying the wrong thing. Then write a list of all the things you wish for – good health, peace, happiness, love, serenity, success. Fold this list up and put it to one side.

2 Sit cross-legged in a quiet place. Put the fear list beside you. In your lap is a bag or pouch filled with runes or pebbles. Draw a rune from the bag and place it next to your first fear. As you place the rune on the paper imagine that this 'fear' is replaced by something from your wish list. Repeat and each time you place a rune on the list imagine you are plucking out the fears that lie deep within you and replacing them with what you love or desire.

3 As you draw and place the runes/stones you begin to feel lighter. You reach deep inside yourself and discover that beneath the shadows of fear and anxiety lies a realm of imagination, fantasy and other worlds. After you have cast all your pebbles or runes for each of your fears, you are now ready to trust in your intuition. Take up your wish list and smile.

The dark side of the Moon has light too.

the sun

ARCANUM NINETEEN

Astrological affinity Sun
Keywords Communication,
sharing, happiness, joy • Positive
energy • Creativity and growth •
Accomplishment in love • New
friendship • Feeling intellectually
enlightened • Being the centre of
attention • Believing in yourself •
Honouring your values

The Sun represents all that is the joy of the ego. The Sun has always been worshipped as the source of all life – without it we wouldn't be here.

symbols and meaning

The Sun symbolizes courage, victory, illumination, the truth and intellectual and emotional clarity. The Fool learnt from the Moon that beneath the veil of self-deception there is a deeper hidden truth, a world of imagination and the invisible, a mysterious force that can help us. Now he meets the radiance of the Sun within himself and begins to understand how to play, make a success of life and revel in his own vitality. When you draw this as a daily card, you will feel vibrant and alive. You can accept your own glory, your own greatness and take centre-stage. No more fear of self, only realization of self. The Sun asks us to move on and leave our shadows behind.

position interpretations

As a 'you now' card it's time to communicate your feelings, express your dreams and play with life. This is a positive card and signifies success and happiness. You can accept your friends or partner for who they are, rather than trying to change them. As a 'future' card you can expect to be happier, fun-loving and liberated from past doubts and fears. A fulfilling relationship will begin, not necessarily an intimate one, but one that will have a positive effect on your life. As a 'blockage' card you may be exaggerating how happy you are or only looking at the surface of a relationship. Alternatively you're so concerned about your image or success that you aren't aware of anyone else's needs.

reversed meaning

If the Sun is in the reversed position, you feel everyone is special but you.

you are the sunshine of your life

If the Sun isn't shining then you will have to use your creative imagination for this exercise.

You will need Sunshine, street
You will feel Like a Sun god/goddess
Result Realizing you are someone special

1 Find a cafe or bench and sit for a while. Notice the shadows of other people as they pass by. If it is midday and summertime, you might hardly see their shadows; in winter they'll be long, stretched and distorted, trailing behind like swathes of demon hair.

2 Now look at the people – all with an image of who they think they are, some with low esteem, some with high, but all lit up in the sunlight and all with shadows.

3 Now imagine that the Sun disappears behind a cloud. You have no shadow, so does that mean you have no substance? For a moment you have vanished in a way; you cast no shadow, so how can you be real? You need both your light and your shadow to be uniquely you.

4 Imagine the Sun shines again, you feel the warmth on your arms or face, you feel assured and fearless again. So you have a shadow; so what? Everyone does. You are now filled with self-confidence and the power of a Sun deity, illuminated, bright and brazen. You walk down the road and turn your face to the sky and thank the solar energy for giving you radiant life and feeling the joy that is the world.

You are special.

judgement

It's only human to say 'I don't approve'. But this is unfair Judgement and is unforgiving. The other kind of Judgement is the opposite.

symbols and meaning

In good Judgement we try to find the truth, see the wisdom in weighing up the situation and how we cannot condemn others, nor blame ourselves either. The positive energy of Judgement is that you feel ready to make a choice, or see things in a new light. You let go of the past, hear your calling, or feel reborn and liberated. The Fool has seen his shadowy side in the Moon, he's seen that fear can be replaced with joy, and now he has a feeling of true self-awareness. He forgives his old self, and now makes a choice to fulfil his true potential. When you draw this card as a daily card, you know what you have to do to have your own day of reckoning.

position interpretations

As a 'you now' card, Judgement implies you are now liberating yourself from old attitudes, whether towards a lover, family or patterns of behaviour that haven't been right for you. You have new insight into how to handle your relationships. This is your chance to start afresh, let go of the past and stop feeling guilty for your actions. As a 'future' card you will have to make a decision by facing up to the facts, rather than avoiding them. As a 'blockage' card, you either feel judged by others or feel you are responsible for someone's sense of happiness or lack of it.

ARCANUM TWENTY

Astrological affinity Pluto
Keywords Liberation, judgement,
atonement • Accounting for past
actions • Re-evaluation and
revival • Dropping old values,
embracing new ones • Accepting
things the way they are •
Recognizing your vocation •
Forgiveness of self and others

reversed meaning

If Judgement appears in the reversed position you may be regretting the past, feeling you've done something wrong.

judgement time

Judgement is a strange card. It is hard to fathom from the image whether we are about to be saved or not. We judge the imagery according to our own personal values. In this exercise you are going to create your own Judgement Day Tarot card. It doesn't have to be fancy or clever – you can sketch it, paint it, cut it out, make it bigger or smaller.

You will need Paper, pens, paints, crayons
You will feel Centred
Result Understanding that Judgement is about transformation

1 Get a stiff piece of card the same size as the card on this spread, then cut out photos or images from magazines that give you a sense of what 'Judgement Day' means to you. It might be a sense of vocation or a calling.

2 If you currently feel 'judged' by someone, imagine how that would look as an image. If you feel guilty for something, write it out on the card as an exercise in self-revelation or to cleanse yourself of self-blame. Perhaps you feel unburdened, blameless, cleansed and ready to follow your dream. What would that look like?

3 Whatever you do, this is your chance to redeem yourself by creating the Judgement Day card of your choice.

You have learnt how to choose wisely and take responsibility for that choice.

the world

ARCANUM TWENTY ONE

Astrological affinity Saturn
Keywords Completion, fulfilment,
freedom • Cosmic love • Freedom
from fear • Feeling at one with the
Universe • Reward for hard work
and effort • Celebration of self and
others • Accomplishing goals •
Travelling mentally and physically
• 'The world's my oyster!'

The World symbolizes both the complete person, integrated, whole and self-aware as well as the fulfilment of one's choices or goals.

symbols and meaning

In any layout the World is a positive card; there's always a sense of accomplishment and prosperity. Everything is working for us, dynamic, moving, vibrant and alive as the world itself. The Fool is now living out his true potential and sees that life is meaningful and he has a purpose in it. He has realized that all the different little bits of him, whether negative or positive, make up the wholeness of himself. Likewise, when you draw this card you have a sense of individual value and 'wholeness'.

position interpretations

As a 'you now' card, the World can also mean you've got the perfect partner or vocation and there's no turning back. You know that whatever happens, you have the chance to move on, follow your heart's desire and there are no regrets. As a 'future' card, you can look forward to success in relationships and all creative enterprises. Sometimes this card is interpreted as 'the world is yours'. You're about to embark on a trip of a lifetime or into a new venture. You feel carefree and yet part of the whole. In a sense you are at one with the Universe. As a 'blockage' card, you could be too sure of yourself, or simply indulging in too much wishful thinking. You may need to ask yourself some straight questions and give straight answers. 'Who am I? What do I need to learn? What is my true potential?'

reversed meaning

If the World turns up in a reversed position, you may need to take a more objective look at what you want or the journey you're choosing to take.

digging for treasure

Remember that treasure map you made at the beginning of your journey (see pages 26–27)? Well, now you're going to 'dig up' the 'arca' or secret box.

You will need The treasure island map you created for the Fool
You will feel At one with the Universe, alchemical
Result Knowing the Fool wasn't so crazy after all

1 Unfold the map before you. Reflect on your drawing, identify the points you marked as signposts or clues to the hidden treasure. Consider your own Tarot journey so far. Has it been dangerous or easy? Was it as exhilarating or demanding as the route you plotted on your imaginary desert island? Does it feel similar to how you imagined it would be?

2 So the Fool in you can now face the true Self. With honesty and integrity, this part of the journey is over. You have the treasure in your hands, and what is that treasure if not you? You have discovered yourself through the Tarot, and now you're ready to begin another journey by using the Tarot as a daily practice or to reveal the truth about who you are as you go through your own life journey.

3 Now fold or roll up your treasure map and keep it somewhere safe. From time to time meditate upon it and return to this place where you discovered your own inner gold.

You are the Tarot.

THE MINOR ARCANA

Now that you have a deeper understanding of the archetypal nature of the Major Arcana and worked with each card in depth, it's time to get acquainted with the Minor Arcana.

The Minor Arcana is made up of 56 cards. There are four suits — Swords, Wands, Pentacles and Cups — and 14 cards within each suit numbered Ace (one) through to ten, and then four court cards, the Page, Knight, Queen, King. Though not so powerfully archetypal as the Major Arcana, the cards of the Minor Arcana are, in a sense, the daily escapades, feelings, thoughts and events that the Fool encounters along his journey of self-discovery. In other words, they are the events, things that you feel, think and encounter on your own journey to self-awareness too.

The four elements of Air, Earth, Fire and Water are represented by the four Tarot suits.

what is the minor arcana?

Each suit represents a different aspect of our day-to-day lives. Wands represent our spirit, actions and vision while Pentacles stand for our sense of reality, Swords our state of mind and Cups represent our emotions.

court cards

The four court cards – Page, Knight, Queen and King – usually represent the people in your day-to-day existence. They also reflect the positive and negative qualities of your own personality.

These cards in a spread will tell you which roles or abilities you are 'unconsciously asking' other people to act out for you. For example, I might fall in love with someone who's witty and wise, but I'm unaware of the quality within myself. You hate Joe Bloggs because he's so critical, but in effect you're disowning your own inner critic. So people 'out there' are often important life-changing catalysts in our lives.

Whether Earth Mother (Queen of Pentacles) or ambitious achiever (King of Wands), the court cards are simply a reflection of the self and the kind of role you are acting out or 'getting someone else to act out for you' at the time of the reading.

kings

All four Kings represent dynamic energy. They symbolize the power and charismatic nature of yourself as seen in others. They can appear in life as male authority or father-figures.

queens

The Queens represent the power of femininity. They often appear in your life as queenly, mothering or bossy women.

knights

Knights express extremes of the suit's quality. They have an immature attitude and represent the best and worst of the suit's energy. For example, the Knight of Wands is charming, but totally insensitive.

pages

These have a light-hearted energy. Pages represent the playful spirit of the energy of the suit, and the child within you. Pages can appear in our lives as the opportunist or the immature colleague we loathe at work.

the numbered cards

Many Tarot decks don't have images for the numbered cards and use only the number and a series of pips to denote which is which. The deck used in this book will help you to interpret the numbered cards more easily, but the simple numerology keywords will help you to interpret them too. Basically, numbered cards represent events, activities, encounters and themes in everyday life.

number association

Take up the Ace through to Ten of any of the suits and lay them down in a line. Then write down in your journal a key word for each number as below and by association thread your own words into your list as you gaze at the images. Don't forget, this is just for the number association, not the suit; you'll find out how to interpret the suits on the following pages.

Number	Key word
Ace or One	Unity
Two	Negotiation
Three	Communication
Four	Stability
Five	Versatility
Six	Compassion
Seven	Intuition
Eight	Motivation
Nine	Action
Ten	Endings and beginnings, fulfilment

swords

Keywords Thought, information, illusion, logic

getting to know swords

1 Take up the four court cards and place them in front of you. Observe them and decide if you feel comfortable or uneasy with any of them.

2 Next, take up the numbered cards and lay them out in front of you. These cards represent our 'conscious' sense of being separate in the world. Choose any cards that stand out for you; which do you like and which make you feel uncomfortable. These qualities may well be current 'Sword' issues in your life, so check the keywords briefly to start learning to understand how these operate.

Swords represent our state of mind and are associated with the element of Air in astrology. This suit is concerned with our rational approach to life; in fact we tend to rely on logic and intellect to solve problems.

We all make decisions based on logic, so why does this suit's imagery seem so sad? This logical approach doesn't always sort out our problems and can make life even more complex. Often the intellect creates more heartaches than does the soul. Ironically, Swords indicate that too much rationalizing can lead us away from the truth of our feelings. We have illusions and it is these illusions — whether principles, ideals or assumptions — that the Swords 'cut through'. Swords are double-edged; they remind us that our self-deceit, illusions and fears must be faced and that the mind must work with the wisdom of the heart.

But Swords are neither all negative or all positive; like any card it depends on your circumstances and the value you place on that quality. For example, being 'smart' can be positive if you're smart enough to know when to take an opportunity, but can be negative if you think someone's too 'smart' for their own good. We unconsciously 'dress' the meaning of the cards with our own value judgements.

ace of swords

Keywords Clarity, honesty, objectivity • Resolving a problem • Facing facts •
Knowing the way forwards • Cutting through illusion • Analysing your motives

This card implies that something needs to be expressed – an idea, a new
challenge or a time for honesty. When you draw this as a daily card, it's time
to be logical and firm. This card requires real inner honesty, too. In the 'you
now' position, it's timely to resolve a problem with clarity; its also time
to face the facts. As a 'future' card, challenges will be coming your way
soon, but this will open you up to more opportunities. As a 'blockage'
card, you're letting your head rule your heart.

two of swords

Keywords Blind to the truth • Denial • Blocked feelings • Being unavailable •
Putting up barriers • Pretending one thing, feeling another

The Two of Swords symbolizes one of our biggest problems – denial and
putting up barriers. Whether in a relationship or simply one's own self-
expression, this card reflects those moments when we pretend indifference
or split off from our feelings and hope they'll go away. If you draw this in
the 'you now' position, you are avoiding the truth of a situation or how you
feel. As a 'blockage' card, the Two of Swords suggests you're not only cut off
from your self, but also cutting yourself off from someone else.

three of swords

Keywords Broken heart • Discovering a painful truth • Feeling let down •
Betrayal • Hurting someone else • Fear of losing • Feeling alone

This is a complex card; the imagery is powerful and there is often a sudden
realization that something's not as it should be. This is because we're usually
not 'looking' for these kind of experiences in our lives, and why should
we? So the positive influence of the Three of Swords asks you to get to the
heart of any difficult situation and sort it out. Its negative associations
(given above) are more common in the 'you now' and 'future' positions.
However, the double-edge of this particular Sword is that if you do try to
look objectively at your fears or sense of loss, you will work things out. It's
time for a reality check.

four of swords

Keywords Repose, contemplation • Taking a new approach • Coming to terms with things • Finding some space • Slowing down • Having a break

The warrior on this card is taking a break; he's laid down his sword and come to terms with what is. Similarly, when you draw this card in a 'you now' position, it's important to take more time to think things through before you make any decisions. Don't let anyone push you for answers. Alternatively, your own past may be preventing you from moving on. You may be paralyzed by your own fears and self-doubt, so look at these in the cold light of day. As a 'blockage' card, constructive communication is what's needed; don't think you can work it out alone.

five of swords

Keywords Defeat, hollow victory, accepting limitations • No-win situation • Only thinking of yourself • Experiencing hostility • Looking after number one

The Five of Swords isn't difficult to interpret if you remember you will either project your current reactions to 'conquest' and 'defeat' on to the card. Do you identify with the knight who seems to have won a hollow victory or with the two forlorn characters who've given up hope? In the 'you now' position, a more positive reading would suggest you can conquer all your fears in spite of the odds. As a 'blockage' card, the Five of Swords indicates there is hostility or dishonourable feelings in your life.

six of swords

Keywords Recovery, travel, new departure • Leaving the past behind • Getting over difficulties • Being more positive about life • Healing experience

In the 'you now' position, the Six of Swords indicates you're moving out of troubled waters. You're unsure of what's going to happen next, but you can see the way ahead. This card usually indicates you're going through some kind of psychological healing process. When this card is in the 'future' position you'll soon be rowing away from those choppy waters for an easier route. In the 'blockage' position, life just isn't flowing. You feel bogged down in problems and need to accept that you have to make an effort to make changes.

seven of swords

Keywords Stealth, dishonesty, escape, lone-wolf • Running from the truth • Wanting to be alone • Lying or cheating • Getting away with it

If you draw this card, don't run away from the truth of it. Perhaps you are avoiding someone or have done something that ultimately means the finger of blame will point at you. In the 'you now' position, don't deceive yourself about your actions. Maybe you just want some space to be alone, but haven't admitted it to yourself yet? As a 'blockage' card, your lone-wolf attitude is just making things more difficult for you.

eight of swords

Keywords Self-sabotage, powerlessness • Feeling trapped • Waiting to be rescued • Feeling victimized • Floundering in feeling • Bound by your illusions

The woman of the Eight of Swords is bound and blindfolded yet it's almost as if she isn't trying to break free. When you draw this card in the 'you now' position, you might be hoping someone will come along and rescue you. But no one can rescue us from ourselves. We have to do it alone. The solutions are there if you use the positive energy of Swords and the power of objectivity and clear-thinking. As a 'blockage' card, the Eight of Swords implies that your sense of feeling lost and confused is preventing you from moving on.

nine of swords

Keywords Sleepless nights • Guilt • Overwhelmed with worries • Wishing 'if only' • Regretting the past • Obsessive thinking • Refusing to forgive

The Nine of Swords looks even bleaker than the Eight. Sleepless nights, well we've all had those when our thoughts become obsessive worries and fears. Worry and guilt are often inner causes of pain and this card in the 'you now' position indicates it's timely to look within for the source of these nagging thoughts. Refocus your goals and be honest about your own vulnerability. You may feel there's something wrong, but you don't know what — the Nine of Swords asks you to wake up to what that is. As a 'blockage' card, explore what illusions or worries are immobilizing you.

ten of swords

Keywords Enlightenment, martyrdom, turning point • Exaggerated self-pity • Feeling life can't get any worse • Darkest moment before the dawn

The Ten of Swords looks even more alarming than Nine. But this is a powerful and complex card, and like all Tens, it represents the end of a cycle and the beginning of a new one. It's timely to dump your baggage, say goodbye to the old 'you' and realize that things can only get better. It may seem as if life is against you in the 'you now' position, but feeling a victim won't get you results either. In the 'blockage' position, you're exaggerating your problems and they're probably not as bad as you make out. Or maybe you're playing the victim to have power over someone?

page of swords

Keywords Vigilance, ready for action • Youthful ideas • Research the facts • Challenging lover • Young-at-heart person • Fresh challenges ahead

As a 'you now' card, you're ready for new challenges, they might not be the ones you'd choose, but you're prepared. When you draw this card, ask yourself if you fear challenge or welcome it? Are you like the Page of Swords, ready for anything? Sword challenges usually come in the form of ideas, questions or tasks that stimulate your mind. Open your eyes, don't let emotional investment spoil the truth. As a 'blockage' card, stop deceiving yourself that you know all the answers.

knight of swords

Keywords Self-assured, incisive • Frank, impetuous, critical • Indiscreet • Powerful intellect • Analyse the situation • Cuts off from feeling

The Knight of Swords represents extremes of the suit's energy. Analyse your underlying motivations for siding with one or the other. As a 'you now' card, are you about to rush headlong into doing something without a thought? Alternatively, are you being intellectual, cool and incisive in handling the issue concerning the spread? As a 'blockage' card, you may be letting your head rule your heart, or someone else is so bossy that you don't have a chance to speak up. The Knight can also manifest as a demanding lover or someone who won't take no for an answer.

queen of swords

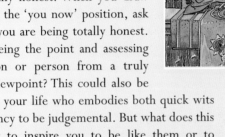

Keywords Direct, unpretentious, astute •
Getting to the point • Honest and quick-
witted • Lively intellect • Don't take life too
seriously • Judgemental person

The positive aspects of the Queen of
Swords are intellectual savvy, the ability
to be astute, reach a conclusion quickly
and be totally honest. When you draw
this card in the 'you now' position, ask
yourself if you are being totally honest.
Are you seeing the point and assessing
the situation or person from a truly
objective viewpoint? This could also be
someone in your life who embodies both quick wits
but a tendency to be judgemental. But what does this
mean? Is it to inspire you to be like them or to
remind you to not take life so seriously and drop the
judgemental attitude?

king of swords

Keywords Articulate, just, assertive,
analytical • Actively gets to grips with the
situation • High standards • Patriarchal
values • Capable and intellectually adept

The energy of the King is more active
than that of the Queen, so when you
draw the King of Swords, you can pit
your wits against others, involve
yourself in a mental debate, diligently
research an issue or challenge others
with your ideas. Someone may act as
catalyst to activate those qualities within
you. As a 'blockage' card, either
someone is squashing you intellectually
or you are too intolerant of others.

who are they?

1 Make a list of the people
  who you think might be like
  the four Sword characters.
  Under each write a positive
  and a negative attribute. The
  Queen of Swords might only
  be interested in her own power,
  for example, yet her good
  quality is that she is capable
  of making swift decisions.

2 Now direct your attention to
  yourself. Can you identify
  with any of these characters?
  Where are your Sword people
  within you? Write them down
  in your journal.

wands

Keywords Will, vision, desire,
energy, drive

getting to know wands

The following exercise may help you understand how this fire energy appears in your life.

1 Imagine you are a hidden camera inside a coffee machine. People assemble here, pressing buttons and jiggling their coins.

2 You look out and see fingers pressing buttons. Notice the loud people, the ones who are in a rush or want to be centre-stage. Notice how they seem to know there's a hidden camera. They come up close and search for you, the camera. In fact the Wands are looking for you. Can you handle that kind of heat? Action isn't confined to antics around the coffee machine, but it's a good start.

Wands are linked to the astrological element of Fire and are also known as Clubs, Sceptres, Rods or Batons. Their long fiery brands or branches of trees with sprouting shoots represent the spark of life and new growth.

This suit describes daily events or affairs where we are in the process of actively engaging in life; it is about the creative process and how we go out into the world to initiate something. If you draw a majority of Wands in a layout you're impatient and ready for adventure. But they also represent other fiery qualities such as impulsiveness and impatience.

The fire signs Aries, Leo and Sagittarius look forward to the future, and similarly these cards imply you are now looking for the next goal or activating the process of moving ahead. Most of these cards show people seeking, looking, questing or contemplating their quest before they set off towards their goal. Wands reveal the motivational aspects of our daily life but also show how we must first have imagination or vision before we can generate action.

ace of wands

Keywords Creative vision, originality, adventure • Be passionate about life •
Act on your inspiration • Have self-belief • Sexual initiative

This card isn't just about thinking great thoughts like the Ace of Swords; it's about acting upon them and making them real. In the 'you now' position you know the way forwards and it's timely to go. Great opportunities are on offer in the 'future' position, and you will have to show your true talents or potential. In love issues, this card says 'get on with it, and enjoy the fun'. In the 'blockage' position, the Ace of Wands indicates you must be aware of your limitations.

two of wands

Keywords Courage, personal power • Not being afraid to prove a point •
Widening your perspective • Pioneering spirit • Taking a risk without fear •
Seizing the moment

The kind of power you have when you draw this card in the 'you now' position is very human. It's a blend of personal spirit and that human need to conquer, achieve or prove you're unstoppable. Take care if you get this in the 'blockage' position. It's one thing feeling you have the world in your hands, but you have to ground your inspired thinking and stop thinking you're divine. As a 'future' card, you're about to persuade others of your talents or show you mean business.

three of wands

Keywords Exploration, foresight • Starting a new journey • Seeking the truth •
Looking for something different • Visionary ideas • Seeing how best to act

Rather like the figure on the card, you're gazing across the sea ready to embark on a voyage of a lifetime. There's no looking back, only forwards and when you draw this card in the 'you now' position get ready to pack or at least to prepare yourself for the unknown, and with a little foresight work out your route in advance. It's not so much about risk-taking, but setting off with a plan, map, provisions and, like any explorer, being ready for anything. As a 'blockage' card, you're so concerned with what's in store in the future that you're not realizing the facts of the present situation.

four of wands

Keywords Joy, celebration, freedom • Freeing yourself from responsibilities • Social enjoyment • Dumping emotional baggage • Thrills and spills

This is the card everyone wants to have. It's all about celebration and excitement. Even though the two figures on the card aren't exactly dancing around, they're preparing for the social fun ahead. When you draw this card in the 'you now' position the chances are you're excited and ready for action. You're ready to set off on a new romantic adventure or just dance for the joy of being alive. As a 'blockage' card, you're more concerned with social whirls than your own self-development.

five of wands

Keywords Minor setbacks, rivalry • Competition • Trying to defend yourself unsuccessfully • Irritating events • Hassled • Frustrating circumstances

When you look at this card, it's hard to know who's going to win. Similarly when you draw this card, you feel as if you're not sure whether you're being attacked for your views or the world is just against you in some way. Things go wrong, the day isn't what it seems (as a daily card). In the 'you now' position everyone seems more interested in themselves than you. Alternatively, you're at odds with yourself, and what you think you want is not what you actually need. As a 'blockage' card, you feel persecuted by others but playing the scapegoat won't you get anywhere.

six of wands

Keywords Victory, pride • Taking it all in your stride • Looking after number one • Being too arrogant to admit the truth • Superiority complex

There are two kinds of pride – one is based on healthy self-esteem and integrity, and a knowledge that you're only human but you've done something worthwhile. The other kind of pride comes before a fall, and is also know as 'hubris'. When you draw this card be very careful you know which one is which. Humility is called for but you can pat yourself on the back if you are sure you have been fair to everyone else. As a 'blockage' card, self-inflation or a superiority complex is stopping you from following your true path.

seven of wands

Keywords Defiance, assertion, purpose • Standing your ground • Being resolute • Sticking to your guns • Strength against adversaries

Defiance and self-belief are indicated, and it's time to make a stand and fight for your rights or opinion. By creating resistance, you're actually creating new assertive energy. You might have to face criticism or literally defend yourself against a verbal or emotional attack. In the 'you now' position you're encouraged to say 'no' rather than compromise. Be honest about what you truly want and take action. In the 'blockage' position, you're battling with your conscience or you're finding it difficult to resist other people's demands.

eight of wands

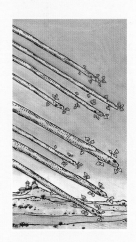

Keywords News • Quick developments • Making intentions clear • Everything up in the air • Sorting out priorities • Resolving unfinished business

With the Eight of Wands everything seems up in the air, there's a whoosh of energy; it's timely to make your move and either get things underway or be prepared for things to happen faster than you had intended. When you draw this as a 'you now' card, you might be rushing ahead with your plans but act now, and things will work out as you wish. Don't hesitate and come down to Earth and ground your ideas or plans. In a 'future' position, be prepared for news or an important message. As a 'blockage' card, you're so obsessed with shifting the goalposts, you'll never get a goal.

nine of wands

Keywords Feeling defensive and cautious • Preparedness • Expecting the worst • Persisting • Remembering past hurts • Stay alert to your self

The Nine of Wands reminds us that we've all been through some scrapes and feel emotionally wounded at times. But now is the time to be prepared and get on with life, but not to the extent where we are constantly looking behind us. This card says be alert, but to both your strengths and weaknesses. As a 'you now' card, persevere and refuse to take 'no' for an answer. As a 'blockage' card, you're so obsessed with what went wrong, you expect the worst to happen.

ten of wands

Keywords Uphill struggle, heavy burden • Feeling you are to blame • Resigned to being a workhorse • Taking on too much • Struggling with workload • Feeling accountable

When you draw the Ten of Wands you may be going through a difficult struggle at work or just taking on too much. This card says cut down on your responsibilities, lighten the load and consider revamping your lifestyle. Whatever else, the burdens of work or of your emotions are taking over your life and you really need to find more time to play. In the 'future' position, there may be some heavy burdens ahead, but you'll deal with them. As a 'blockage' card, it's your willingness to give to all and sundry that's stopping you from moving on.

page of wands

Keywords Creativity, fresh ideas • A messenger • Willing to try something new • Charming admirer • Be courageous • Child-like exuberance • Showing your enthusiasm

The Page of Wands can quite simply be someone young, light-hearted and charming who comes into your life to remind you of your own inner 'Peter Pan'. When you draw this card as a 'you now' card it's time to be inspired and creative about your life, or you'll have chances for new romance. In the 'blockage' position you're so enthusiastic about someone new, that you're ready to give up on your own beliefs.

knight of wands

Keywords Impetuous, foolhardy • Adventurous • Gift of the gab/braggart • Charming/insensitive • Seductive/lustful • Accomplished/exaggerates • Rogue

A charming rogue can be fun to have around if you're looking for new romance, but not so welcome when you're already involved. This card is all about vivacity, daring and passion. In the 'you now' position you need to be more outgoing and seductive, and express your daring streak. This could also imply a knight in shining armour who sweeps you off your feet! In the 'blockage' position, either you're infatuated with a heartbreaker or if it's not a relationship spread then the chances are you're just being too impulsive.

queen of wands

Keywords Self-assured, attractive • A woman who knows where she's going • Sexually accomplished • Never fazed • Energetic and busy

The Queen of Wands doesn't worry about what people think of her. She's attractive, focused and easy-going. She knows exactly how to keep herself full of vitality and has complete faith in her own abilities. When you draw this card, ask yourself if you are like her. If not, then it's time to develop those magnetic qualities in yourself. Enjoy your vitality and attraction factor. If a 'blockage' card, there's a woman in your world who makes you feel small and unattractive. Or you're so dedicated to looking good your relationships are suffering.

king of wands

Keywords Charismatic, inspiring • Dramatic, bold • Setting an example • Powerful leader • Role model • Willing to take a risk • Boldly confident

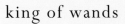

This King is totally confident about himself and knows he's charismatic. He could appear in your life as a male authority figure or this card asks you to act like this king. Be bold, create confidence in others, be assertive when you have to be. The inspirational energy of the King in the 'you now' position says put on a performance and shine. As a 'blockage' card, someone in power is holding you back, or you have power issues yourself that need to be addressed.

pushy people

1 Imagine you're sitting at a boardroom table. You have asked each of the four court card personalities to present an advertising pitch for a new eco-friendly car. What would they come up with? Try to see the very different qualities of their personalities coming through the sales pitch. Which of their ideas do you like best?

2 Do you feel comfortable with these pushy people or would you rather invite more laid-back characters to your company? Record how you feel in your Tarot journal.

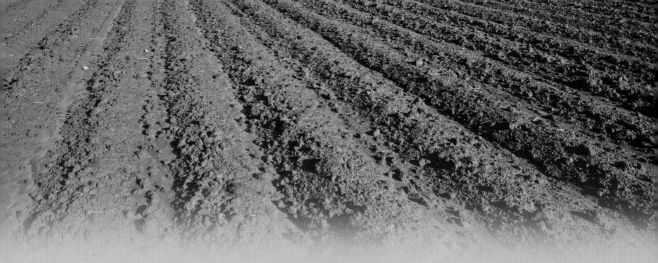

pentacles

The suit of Pentacles is concerned with 'substance'. Like the Earth signs in astrology – Taurus, Virgo and Capricorn – Pentacles represents the tangible things of life that give us a sense of security.

imagined sensation

1 You're going to try to experience some of your senses in your head. First try to smell a rose or jasmine in your head. Very difficult.

2 Then imagine being kissed. Is it a light caress of the lips, or a deep passionate kiss that sweeps you away? Not easy to remember experientially.

3 Perhaps more difficult is imagining you can hear a sound you've never heard before. What does a hummingbird sound like or a watermelon being cracked open?

This exercise reveals that our sensory experience of the world is as important as our intellectual or emotional one. Trust in the Pentacles to lead you there.

Pentacles (also known as Discs and Coins in some decks) tells us on a most basic level about the concrete world. The suit of Pentacles represents our sensory perception of the world and how we connect and interact with it. Like any of the other cards, each Pentacles has two sides to its 'coin'. What is your perception of reality? Are you driven by power that money can bring? Or does the substance of spirituality appeal to you? This suit also represents the things and people that define or shape us into who we are.

Spread the cards out in ascending order across the table or floor and as you look at them, remove any that have a specific resonance with you, good or bad. Do you know any people who might be examples of the court cards. How do you react to the Queen of Pentacles? Think about yourself in the material world first. Are you organized at work. How do you deal with money? Are you obsessed with materialism or don't really care? Notice how most of the numbered cards show people 'doing' something in the world.

ace of pentacles

Keywords Results, prosperity, abundance • Being realistic • Power to get what you want • Being grounded and focused • Seeing a way to achieve a goal • Trusting in the situation

Whenever you draw this card in the 'you now' position it reminds you that its time to be realistic about what you want, but also if you make an effort and come down to Earth, you'll succeed in your ventures. In the 'future' position, there may even be a gift coming your way, an opportunity or a realistic offer. Use your talents to follow up new resources. It's not about dreaming what might be, but doing what is.

two of pentacles

Keywords Flexibility, juggling, balancing • Juggling with the options • Going with the flow • Feeling good about your skills • Ability to adapt • Dealing with several problems at once • Open to change • Having a laugh

The Two of Pentacles reminds you to be adaptable in the material world. Events and people aren't always under our control, but if we're flexible and willing to adapt, we'll also produce results. In the 'you now' position, you're feeling confident in your abilities or it's timely to sort out any relationship differences. Have a laugh, don't take life so seriously. In the 'blockage' position, you might be taking on too much and feel the need to take a break.

three of pentacles

Keywords Co-operation, teamwork, skill • Getting the job done • Professional growth • Being aware of your skills • Being obsessed with detail • Feeling competent

Even though you'd like to do things your way, it's probably better to share the load with others. You can now prove yourself, but don't turn away and think you don't need other people. Combine your own efforts with others and succeed. In the 'you now' position, it is your competence and professional growth that is now in focus. As a 'blockage' card, you're too dependent on what others think to dare to do your own thing.

four of pentacles

Keywords Possessive, mean • Greedy • Resisting change • Tight-fisted and mercenary • Small-minded • Materialism as a source of manipulation

This card shouts out 'you can't have it, it's mine!'. This is materialism at its worst. We can all be possessive, so when you draw this card in the 'you now' position, check you're not trying to control other people through money or possessions. The positive side of the Four of Pentacles is that if you are involved in a uncontrollable situation, you can now create order in your world. As a 'blockage' card, someone is controlling you or you're feeling tied down by financial necessity.

five of pentacles

Keywords Hardship, victim mentality • Material difficulties • Feeling excluded • Neglecting your needs • Soul-searching • Sense that something's missing

Whenever you draw the Five of Pentacles there is a sense of 'lack' in your life. It might be material security, or spiritual connection or a feeling that you don't feel 'rich'. This card often turns up when we feel let down or when we've become a victim. The positive aspect of this card is that if your life is lacking something, then you must go out and discover what that is. This is also the mentality of someone who sees the glass half-empty rather than half-full. In the 'blockage' position you are so wrapped up in your feeling of inadequacy that you can't see your way forward.

six of pentacles

Keywords Generosity, having/not having • Loss/gain • Giving/taking • Domination/submission • Teaching/learning • Two sides of the same coin

A paradoxical card, the Six of Pentacles asks us to understand the polarity of 'to have and to have not'. This card suggests that sometimes in our gains we lose and sometimes in our losses we win. The Six of Pentacles also asks you to consider whether your generosity or kindness is all that it seems. Are you gaining from giving approval? Are you buying someone's love? Who has the power in a relationship? Always check your underlying motives when you draw this card. In the 'blockage' position be equally vigilant, and see which particular side of the 'coin' you are actually on.

seven of pentacles

Keywords Evaluation, assessment • Seeing fruits of labour • Prepared for a new goal • Taking stock • Taking a break • Where or what next?

The Seven of Pentacles says it's time to take a reality check when in the 'you now' position. You've worked hard so far, you've done everything right, and now it's one of those moments to pause, reflect and evaluate where you go from here. You know that you can go a little further, perhaps even branch out into new territory and sow a few more seeds. In a 'blockage' position, you feel you're at a crossroads and don't know which way to turn.

eight of pentacles

Keywords Diligence, proficiency • Dedicated to the job • Repetitive work or situation • Perseverance paying off • Training for a new skill • Getting down to the nitty-gritty

When this card appears in a spread, you are being reminded to 'get on with it' whatever 'it' is. If you act with discipline and diligence you'll be rewarded. It may not necessarily be a practical issue or work-related, so if you were asking a relationship question, then interpret this card as a time to find out as much as you can and absorb yourself in those experiences. Repairs and renewals in the self-awareness department come to mind here, especially if in the 'blockage' position.

nine of pentacles

Keywords Accomplishment, self-reliance • Having a comfortable lifestyle • Enjoying the finer things of life • Being responsible • Inner sense of security • Financial or material resourcefulness • Having grace

When you draw the Nine of Pentacles you're both designer of your own destiny but also of your instincts and emotions. In fact, you're accomplished in the art of sensual skills, material self-reliance and the ability to show restraint. In the 'you now' position, it's timely to ask yourself if you welcome your independent attitude and this card also indicates your most important duty is to yourself. As a 'blockage' card you may be so confident and self-disciplined that you won't let anyone get close to you.

ten of pentacles

Keywords The good life, conventional values • Tradition, wealth • Seeking affluence • Enjoying abundance • Sticking to the tried and tested

This is where it all happens in the big wide world. When you draw this card in the 'you now' position there's a feeling of abundance and material contentment around you. Alternatively, you may be seeking security and have a desire for a solid stable family life. The Ten of Pentacles is also concerned with conventional values and sticking to the status quo. In the 'blockage' position, you may be so stuck in your ways you daren't take a risk or try a more radical approach to life.

page of pentacles

Keywords Realistic aims, practical approach • Focus and progress • Proving you're reliable • Having a good effect • Seeing a window of opportunity

When you draw this card in the 'you now' position it's time to get practical and involve yourself with a new project. This is a 'hands on' card, so whether it's a relationship issue or a career matter, this card has a 'let's get on with the job' feel about it. The Page can also be represented by someone you know who is practical, diligent and organized. As a 'blockage' card, it indicates that it is great to be such a whizz-kid but you're so focused on your goals you can't see your real priorities.

knight of pentacles

Keywords Persistent, hardworking, unadventurous • Realistic or gloomy • Inflexible or dedicated • Cautious or afraid to take a risk • Effort but no passion • Slow to get involved in love

This is one mixed-up Knight. When you draw this card ask yourself whether you identify with his gloomy, pessimistic, defensive nature or his determined, dedicated, hard-working one? This card reminds you it's time to knuckle down and get on with the job. The work could be improving a relationship or taking up a new career, but don't fear the effort involved. In a 'blockage' position, the Knight of Pentacles indicates you need to overcome your doom-and-gloom approach to the issue involved. As a 'future' or outcome card, embrace your potential and refuse to quit.

queen of pentacles

Keywords Earth Mother • Nurturing and warm-hearted • Desire to help others • Creative and resourceful • Trustworthy and loyal • Unpretentious and sensible

The Queen of Pentacles is nurturing, a sensual yet devoted mother type. She's always there when you need her and her greatest joy is looking after other people and making them happy. Do you envy her or admire her? Is she someone in your life right now who can inspire you? Whoever she represents, as a 'you now' card, it's time to become a dependable friend and lover or find your compassionate side. As a 'blockage' card the Queen signifies you're looking after everyone else at your own expense.

king of pentacles

Keywords Reliable, enterprising • Philanthropic • Charismatic • Financial adviser • Resolute • Has the 'Midas' touch

This King knows he's untouchable. He's organized, sorted out all practical matters and is materially secure. He has few hang-ups and is totally reliable. When you draw this card in the 'you now' position, you have an instinct for making a success out of any venture, whether material or emotional. If you feel this confident, skilful energy is lacking in your life, then this is your chance to make the necessary changes without too much effort. As a 'blockage' card you may be so obsessed with your career that your relationship is suffering.

dinner with the court cards

1 Imagine you've invited these four characters to dinner. You've created the perfect meal, lavish wine, expensive tableware, the ultimate in natural products and superb cooking.

2 How would each of them react to the meal afterwards? Write their departing scripts and try to get a different approach (all influenced by Pentacle energy) for each of these characters. For example, the Knight might say, 'I'm stuffed, think I'd better go and lie down', or 'Must get back to work now. Hey, don't waste the prawn heads, I'll give them to my cat.'

cups

enter the world of feelings

1 Try to imagine all the people in the world and what they're feeling at this very moment. At every moment, as you meditate on every place on Earth simultaneously, imagine people making love, dying, being born, talking, eating, wanting, envying, missing others, crying, feeling feelings that we all share. So universal is the feeling of feeling that it will overcome you.

2 If you fear feeling the feelings of the Universe and try to shut it out you will never understand the energy of the Cups. If you let yourself bask in the infinity of universal relating, the Cups will touch you this way. Record your reactions in your Tarot journal.

Most Tarot readers are comfortable interpreting this suit because Cups seem directly concerned with relationship issues. Like the astrological Water signs Cancer, Scorpio and Pisces, Cups represent our feelings, emotions and our relationships with other people and the world itself.

Also known as Chalices, Cups remind us that beyond our own ego world is the 'world' out there and how we relate to life. Always interpret these cards as the way you perceive others, the effects others have on you and vice versa, and how this suit can give you indications of love, romance and feelings involved in any issue. The only problem is that Cups have positive and negative energies. Learning to put your own feelings aside when interpreting these cards is quite an art.

Spread out the suit of Cups in chronological order, look at each card in turn and think what it might mean to you without checking up on the interpretations. Think about how you react to each card. With the court cards, think about people you know who are sensitive, emotional or compassionate. Are they like these characters, and can you identify with any of them yourself? Next, think about your own feelings. Do you associate yourself with the feeling world at all, or prefer life to be logical and orderly. Are you indifferent to the energy of the cards or do you feel strongly about any of them? Look at the numbered cards and notice that they are all people 'relating' to the world and are engaged in their feelings and reactions to what is happening around them.

ace of cups

Keywords Romance • Deeper feelings • Expressing love • In touch with your
emotions • Falling in love with love • Desire for a deeper connection • An offer

When you draw the Ace of Cups, a new romance or a deeper involvement
is signified. As a 'you now' card, you might be falling in love with
someone or are infatuated with the idea of love itself. If you're already
attached, this card suggests you want to develop a deeper bond between
you. Check how in touch you are with your feelings as a daily card. Is it
time to open up and reveal all to someone? As a 'blockage' card, you're
letting your feelings take over from the reality of what's happening. This
card can also indicate you're about to be offered a gift or something that
will bring about new opportunities.

two of cups

Keywords Connection, attraction • Moving closer • Sexual attraction •
Establishing a bond • Declaring a truce • Putting the past behind you

This card indicates the bonding nature of a relationship at it's best – when
you stare into each other's eyes and know you can't resist each other. As a
'future' card, the Two of Cups signifies a magnetic attraction between you
and someone new. As a 'you now' card you're sexually attractive, able to
commit yourself or willing to let bygones be bygones. As a 'blockage'
card, you're so wrapped up in your 'twosome' that you're excluding other
others who could help you, or not able to stand alone.

three of cups

Keywords Team spirit, friendship • Exuberance, celebration • Part of a group
• Sharing good feelings • Getting together and networking • Community spirit

When you draw the Three of Cups you have to share your feelings with
more than just a partner, you have to give out goodness all around you. In
the 'you now' position, this card indicates you're blessed with the feel-
good factor and it's time to celebrate with friends or join in the fun. This
card asks you how well you get on in a group situation? Do you find it
easy? Would you prefer to do things alone? As a 'blockage' card you're
spending so much time celebrating that you can't sort out your priorities.

four of cups

Keywords Introspection, self-doubt • Taking things personally • Giving little
away • Not seeing what's on offer • Lacking initiative • Taking time to reflect

There are times when we're so self-absorbed that we can't see what's on
offer. When you draw this card as a daily card, perhaps you are taking things
too personally or are so apathetic that you can't make an effort to do
anything. This suggests you need to open your eyes and heart to what is
genuinely there for you. This card can suggest in the 'you now' position that
you're in need of time to reflect and question your motives. As a 'blockage'
card, you're so negative about yourself that you're missing the key solution.

five of cups

Keywords Loss, regret • Emotional confusion • Feeling sad and grieving •
Regrets over lost opportunities • Change in priorities • Resistance to change

Loss is a very emotive word. We feel uncomfortable at the thought of
losing anything, whether a key, CD or worse, a partner, lover, friend or
family member. Our emotional response also triggers off a familiar fear
mechanism. If we lose something, then surely we'll be alone and
vulnerable again? But loss can be positive if we understand that it initiates
change and growth. What we have lost will be replaced with something
new. Loss can generate new insights and opportunities. As a 'blockage'
card you're so obsessed with your loss you can't see what is to be gained.
The more we hang on to our loss, the longer it takes to move on.

six of cups

Keywords Nostalgia • Playfulness • Goodwill • Sentimental thoughts •
Childhood memories • Doing a good turn • Having a clear conscience

When you draw the Six of Cups, you're no longer in a state of emotional
turmoil as with Five; you are filled with blissful thoughts and a feeling
that all's well with the world. As a 'you now' card you're playful and yet
sentimental about the past. In fact, you're in touch with your inner child
and can forget all the fears, worries and anxieties of adulthood. As a
'blockage' card, however, you're being too naive or living in cloud-
cuckoo land.

seven of cups

Keywords Wishful thinking, self-indulgence • Too much choice • Fantasizing about what you can achieve • High expectations • Putting off the inevitable

There are several options for interpreting this card as a 'you now' or daily card! First, that you have too many choices and you're indecisive. Second, that you're too self-indulgent to make any effort and think things will just happen without your input, and third, you're living under an illusion of your own achievements. When you draw this card, think honestly about these meanings. Are you hoping for something you know is impossible? Are you feeling disorganized or procrastinating? As a 'blockage' card, you've got so many options you can't think clearly.

eight of cups

Keywords Moving on • Exploring a new lifestyle • Leaving behind a difficult situation • Trying to find a deeper meaning • Search for inner awareness

The Eight of Cups always indicates a time of change. There is a feeling that things must shift, that something is not quite right about the place we're in. This card often signifies that it is time to move on from the old you, and take up the new you. Things are out of balance as suggested by the stacking of the cups on the card, and it is a chance for you to restore harmony within yourself. Change produces anxiety and getting out of a rut can be the hardest thing we do. As a 'blockage' card, it is your very fear of moving on that is creating current difficulties.

nine of cups

Keywords Wish fulfilment • Emotional and sexual satisfaction • Enjoying the good life • Pleased with your achievements • Counting your blessings

Originally, this card was considered to mean 'my wish will now come true'. Similarly, you are now encouraged to enjoy yourself and feel good about being you. A little caution is required, however, when you draw this card in the 'you now' position. If you are basking in some kind of success, take care that your self-esteem doesn't create envy or emotional manipulation. In the 'blockage' position you are so full of yourself you can't see anyone else's point of view.

ten of cups

Keywords Promise of good times to come • Family joy, happiness • Radiating love • Emotional fulfilment • Sexual commitment • Attainable ideals

This card indicates that all is well, that in your search for happiness the energy is positive right now. As a 'blockage' card you may be so determined to find the perfect partner that you haven't realized the key to the love door is right before your eyes. Alternatively, family and friends are preventing you from moving on. As a 'future' card, you will soon see the light and can welcome emotional or sexual commitment to bring balance back to your life.

page of cups

Keywords Romantic feelings • Sensitivity • Being offered love • A younger lover • A flirtatious admirer • Trusting your intuition • Being forgiving

When you draw the Page of Cups, it can indicate a new, younger or maybe even naive lover coming into your life. As a 'you now' card it can imply that you or someone else is acutely sensitive. As a 'blockage' card think about what you have to offer in a current relationship or what is being offered? Is it enough? Are you truly giving with your heart or only because you seek approval? The Page of Cups also represents forgiveness, and it may be that you are about to forgive yourself or someone else and free yourself from the blame game.

knight of cups

Keywords Idealization, over-emotional • In love with love • Temperamental • Exaggerated feelings • Emotional rescue • Victim/saviour relationship

When you draw this card always think about whether the energy is missing in your life or is it overwhelming? In the 'you now' position, the Knight of Cups can either represent someone poetic, gushing and sentimental or a real Knight in shining armour ready to whisk you off your feet. On the negative side, this card can indicate that you or someone else is taking things too personally. You're twitchy, petulant, irritable and take offence easily. As a 'blockage' card, you may be in love with love and not seeing the real 'person' behind the facade.

queen of cups

Keywords Tender-hearted, compassionate
• Feeling moved • Unconditional love •
Knows what it feels like to feel • Willing to
help the underdog

When you draw the Queen of Cups as a
'you now' card, you are full of emotional
empathy and compassion and others will
be attracted to you for that reason.
Alternatively, someone who represents
the qualities of tender-heartedness
will come into your life. As a 'blockage'
card, your emotional involvement with
someone (or being wrapped up in your
own feelings), means you can't see the truth of what's
going on. As a 'future' card, you will soon be more
compassionate with yourself and others.

king of cups

Keywords Stability, wisdom, diplomacy •
Generosity • Keeping your head in a crisis
• Broad-minded and tolerant • Accepting
your limitations • Evaluating a situation

The King of Cups is serious about his
watery kingdom as he sits thoughtfully
on his throne. When you draw this
card in the 'you now' position, you're
ready to make a wise choice or decision
based on your emotionally mature
attitude. Alternatively, a stabilizing
force (whether in the guise of a man or
woman), is about to enter your life and
have a powerful effect on you for the
better. This person offers wisdom and
good advice. As a 'blockage' card you
may be repressing your own feelings.

the court characters in love

1 Try to imagine how each of the
court card characters would act
when they're in love.

2 Record your impressions of
each one in your Tarot journal
or make up a short story
around one of them. Perhaps
choose another court card
from a different suit and
imagine how they might be
attracted to one another.

For example, the Page of Cups
falls head over heels with anyone
who smiles at him, particularly the
cool but poised Queen of Swords.
He sends roses and romantic
messages to her every day. If
she's late for work he's willing to
make up an excuse on her behalf
and would even pretend to be her
if he didn't have a male voice and
the wrong outfit. If she fails to
reply to his message he naively
thinks 'oh well, I forgive her, I
know she is really busy'.

TAROT SPREADS

Tarot spreads are an exciting way to develop your self-awareness, discover more about your relationships as well as offering an intriguing glimpse into the future. And once you have become familiar with the Major Arcana and the Minor Arcana, you will want to stretch your knowledge and insight further by trying some of the following spreads.

working with tarot spreads

The following spreads are designed to enable you to work gradually and with ease from the simplest interpretations through to the more complex. The first spreads concern your daily life and current situation. You might, for example, want to begin with the 'daily practice spread' in order to familiarize yourself with all the cards and how to combine the interpretations for several cards.

Following these are specific spreads concerning relationship issues. The Relationship spread tells you about the 'workings' of the relationship rather than about you. Some spreads can be done on your own or with your partner. Remember if you do interpret cards on your partner's behalf, make sure you're not investing what you want your lover to think, feel or do rather than what the card really means.

The Revelation spreads continue the themes of your personal world, but these are much more detailed and are designed for self-development and deeper understanding. But always think about what the 'future' means to you at the moment you are reading the cards. Remember, the cards reflect you at the moment you select them, so think how the lessons or knowledge revealed in these larger spreads can be applied to you now as well as the future.

Lastly, the spreads for Freeing the Spirit are used to develop your symbolic and psychic awareness through the cards. These spreads are also designed to get in touch with the archetypal nature of the Universe.

Finally, remember that we all want to know 'what the future holds'. This gives us a sense of security and we feel we can control our future rather than be at the hands of fate. This knowledge is actually generated by our own inner desires and these spreads help you to confirm exactly what you already know inside and what you want to happen. That's when you begin to realize that your character IS your destiny.

how to lay out the cards

1 Make sure you are in a quiet, comfortable environment so you can focus and begin to listen to your intuitive voice. Perform your favourite ritual by either lighting a candle or burning incense, and then make sure you have enough space to lay out the cards on the floor or table.

2 Have your Tarot journal beside you so that you can make notes as you go along. Write down your question or issue first so that it's clear in your head. We often distort the original question after laying out the cards.

3 Shuffle and cut the deck in one of the ways recommended on pages 18–19.

4 As you shuffle, focus on the question or issue raised. Then either hold the cards fanned out in one hand face down (easier once you're more experienced), or place them face down on the floor and spread them out in a long line.

5 Next, choose the relevant number of cards for the particular spread. Lay each one face down in the order and position shown in the spread diagram. Once you have laid them all out face down, you can then turn them face up. If any cards have managed to get reversed and you prefer not to use reversed cards, turn these the right way up too. Personally, I prefer all the cards the right way up as there are so many layers of meaning for each card in its upright position.

6 Check the interpretations in this book, perhaps make notes in your journal as you go along as to what YOU think the card means for you. Eventually, you'll be able to read the whole spread as a complete entity, rather than as separate cards.

7 Follow the keyword text for each spread as well as taking note of the accompanying advice.

your present life

Everyday spreads are easy to do and will give you answers to the questions you have about life and how to navigate it successfully. With just three or four card spreads you can delve deeper into your own daily and long-term needs.

what's going on today spread?

This spread is a simple way to get to know the cards on a daily basis. Apart from just drawing one daily card to give you a flavour of the day's events, this easy layout requires little effort and allows you direct experience of the cards' meanings with a little self-questioning. Lay out the three cards as indicated in the diagram.

❶ **What is the important event of the day?**
❷ **What needs attention/action?**
❸ **What do I watch out for?**

sample reading

❶ **Two of Pentacles.** A day when I can cope easily with other people's demands, prove myself flexible and have some fun in the process.

❷ **Page of Swords.** I may be tested by a new challenge and need to be totally honest in all my dealings.

❸ **Knight of Cups.** I must watch out for someone becoming over-sensitive or melodramatic. Me perhaps?

my priorities spread

In daily readings you can also work out what needs attention right now. Sometimes we focus our attention on work rather than relationships and vice versa. This simple spread will get you thinking about what needs to be done first and what things may get in the way of you achieving that particular object or goal for the day. Lay out the five cards as indicated in the diagram.

1. **What is my priority right now?**
2. **What is stopping me?**
3. **What things can I change?**
4. **What things must I accept?**
5. **Outcome?**

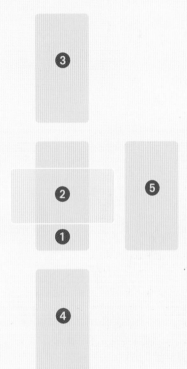

sample reading

1. **The Hierophant.** I must learn to be more discriminating, trust in conventional methods and concentrate on one project.

2. **Page of Wands.** What's stopping me is my desire to go off and be charming or even a little bit mischievous.

3. **Three of Cups.** What I can change is my attitude to teamwork. I must be more willing to get support first, socialize second.

4. **Three of Pentacles.** I must accept that if I really want to build up my image or finalize any projects, I must make more of an effort.

5. **Ace of Cups.** The result is that there will be a really important gift waiting for me in the wings.

my secrets spread

This spread is self-revelatory. It tells you what you really want, but you must be prepared to be totally honest when you interpret this layout. You don't have to do this on a daily basis, but it is useful for making decisions at any time. Our secrets and moods change all the time, and it's only our fear of accepting those inner desires that prevent us from moving on. Lay out the seven cards as indicated in the diagram.

1 **Who/what is my secret love?**
2 **Who/what is my secret hate?**
3 **What is my secret desire?**
4 **What is my secret test?**
5 **What puts me off?**
6 **What motivates me?**
7 **What can I accomplish right now?**

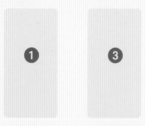
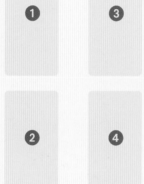
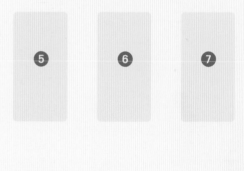

sample reading

1 **Seven of Swords.** My secret love is having time all to myself.

2 **Eight of Wands.** My secret hate is when everything is up in the air and nothing is sorted out.

3 **Justice.** My secret desire is for more equality in my relationship.

4 **Nine of Pentacles.** My secret test is to try to be more self-reliant.

5 **The Magician.** What puts me off are people who achieve more than me.

6 **Eight of Pentacles.** What motivates me is variety in life, a new project.

7 **Two of Wands.** What I can accomplish now is to believe in myself and widen my perspective so I can have more free time and independence.

pros and cons spread

This layout is different from the previous ones because you must choose two cards from the deck first. Look through the pack for the card you like best and the one you don't like at all, and take these two out. You might have to narrow down your choice, and remember that favourites and least favourites can change often, depending on your current situation. Lay out the cards as indicated in the diagram, following the instructions below.

❶ **Pro card.**
❷ **Con card.**
❸ **What do I need to learn?**

1 Lay out the first two chosen cards in the position shown on this page, then shuffle the pack as normal. Now choose one card at random and lay it face down in position 3.

2 Look up the interpretations for your favourite and least favourite cards. Think about why you love one and dislike or even loathe the other. Is the one you don't like particularly significant in some way? Are you repressing this archetypal energy because you fear it, or are you projecting it on to others?

3 Is the card you like also something you aspire to but feel is lacking in your life? Are you living out this quality or merely wishing and hoping for it in your life?

4 Now turn over the third card and discover what you need to learn right now about your pro and con cards.

sample reading

❶ **The Lovers.** My favourite card is the Lovers because it represents the perfect relationship, which is what I long for.

❷ **Three of Swords.** My least favourite card is the Three of Swords because it reminds me of being betrayed and how once someone broke my heart.

❸ **Temperance.** What I need to learn is to see that compromise and moderation are the keys to good relations; that betrayal and love are not mutually exclusive and yet if I am aware of my fear of betrayal, then I can let love back into my life.

The Tarot can help to reveal how you feel about your relationships and their dynamics.

relationships

The Tarot spreads over the next four pages deal with relationships and their complications – the dynamics, how you see each other, feelings engendered and how you sort things out.

relationship dynamic spread

This spread tells you how the relationship between you and someone else is operating. It reveals the current dynamics of the relationship as a separate entity rather than looking at you or your partner individually or by comparison. It's a great spread for getting a sense of what kind of energy is currently being generated, and this is often how other people 'see' you both as a couple, too.

For this spread, you can either use the whole deck or just use the Major Arcana cards for an in-depth interpretation. Lay out the seven cards as indicated in the diagram.

sample reading

1. The Moon. The outward expression of the energy of this relationship is confusing, fluctuating and unstable.

2. The Sun. However, behind the scenes there is good communication.

3. The Star. The relationship's strength is its inspirational dialogue.

4. The Emperor. Its weakness is being too defensive.

5. The Fool. Its reality is its air of child-like fun.

6. The Empress. Sensual and sexy.

7. The Hermit. Do some serious soul-searching for the truth about this relationship if you want to keep it alive.

1. Its energy?
2. Its secret?
3. Its strength?
4. Its weakness?
5. Its reality?
6. Its passion?
7. Key to the future?

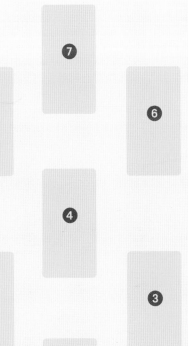

how we see each other spread

You can do this spread on your own or with your partner, but if you do go down the solo route, make sure you are thoroughly honest about interpreting your partner's cards. Don't project your own hopes or fears on to them. It can be handy to have an objective friend to help you interpret. You must decide beforehand who is partner A and who is partner B.

I have deliberately made the people in this spread at extremes of energy to show you how these kind of differences can create openings for good dialogue, and demonstrate whether you are looking for the same things out of a relationship.

For this spread, you can use the whole deck and lay out the six cards as indicated in the diagram.

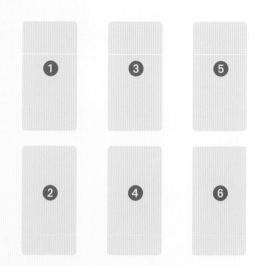

1. **How does A see B?**
2. **How does B see A?**
3. **What does A want from the relationship?**
4. **What does B want from the relationship?**
5. **Where does A believe the relationship is going?**
6. **Where does B believe the relationship is going?**

sample reading

1. **Queen of Cups.** A sees B as caring, compassionate and attractive.

2. **Two of Swords.** B sees A as cool and unavailable.

3. **Two of Cups.** A wants pure romance.

4. **Ten of Pentacles.** B wants stability and commitment.

5. **Nine of Wands.** A isn't sure if will work out, because there is something not quite right between them.

6. **Ten of Wands.** B believes it is going to be an upward struggle to get what B wants.

how to sort it out spread

We all encounter difficulties in our relationships, and often wonder 'what next, where do we go from here, how can we deal with it?'. This spread tells you what the key to the problem is, what to do about it and the future potential. In this example, the question was about sorting out a couple's plans for the future, using six cards.

1 **What is the situation now?**
2 **What is causing the problem?**
3 **What have we forgotten to respect?**
4 **What do we need to express?**
5 **Options available?**
6 **The future potential?**

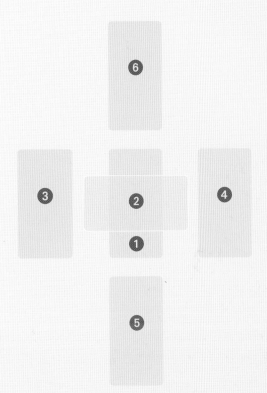

sample reading

1   2   3   4   5   6

1 **Two of Wands.** We are both ready for new adventure or a change of plan.

2 **Seven of Cups.** The problem is that the possibilities seem endless and we can't reach a mutual decision.

3 **Four of Swords.** We have forgotten to respect that we need to take a break and think things through carefully.

4 **Strength.** What we need to express is that we need to face reality. We can't always follow our instincts.

5 **The King of Wands.** The options are simply to mastermind our goals and inspire each other then we'll make progress.

6 **Ace of Pentacles.** Life-changing positive emphasis if we get down to the nitty-gritty.

feelings and resolution spread

This solo layout allows you to be extremely truthful about your current feelings in a relationship. You can explore what you are feeling beneath the surface and then work with that knowledge. Expressing our emotions is cleansing and also leads to acceptance of your flaws as well as your good qualities. The last card represents your resolution to deal with those feelings in the future.

In this layout, which I noted down from a recent client's visit, half of the ten cards chosen were from the Major Arcana, suggesting there were some deep archetypal energies at work in this client's unconscious. There are certain issues she needs to resolve before she can successfully maintain a long-term relationship.

1 **What do I really feel about myself right now?**
2 **What do I fear most for myself in the future?**
3 **What makes me feel angry?**
4 **What makes me feel happy?**
5 **What makes me feel sad?**
6 **What do I hate about you?**
7 **What do I love about you?**
8 **My most secret desire for the two of us?**
9 **What makes me feel vulnerable?**
10 **Resolution?**

sample reading

1 **Knight of Swords.** I feel I'm too headstrong and impatient.

2 **The Hermit.** I'm worried I'm going to do the same old thing over again, repeat bad habits or behaviour that I've tried to leave behind.

3 **Ace of Cups.** Falling in love too easily; I just can't seem to help myself.

4 **Five of Wands.** Unexpected challenges, a little unpredictability and excitement.

5 **Death.** The parting of the ways when a relationship has served its purpose.

6 **Seven of Cups.** I hate the way you're always so optimistic and then get let down and blame everyone else.

7 **The Hanged Man.** I love the way you can see life from any old angle.

8 **The Tower.** My secret desire is that we split up; it sounds odd but it would create movement and change that I secretly want.

9 **Five of Cups.** Problem is, as soon as I'm alone I feel really vulnerable without someone.

10 **The High Priestess.** I resolve to trust my intuition more and try to communicate my feelings to myself and to others.

revelations

The next two spreads are helpful if you are prepared to be honest with yourself and you want to delve deeper into what you want from your life.

what do I need spread

The Tarot can help us to know what we truly need and want in life, and then take action accordingly.

This is a simple yet revealing spread when you're not sure what you need in life or where you're going. Be honest with yourself and remember your needs and wants change with time, so you can do this spread quite regularly.

There are five cards in this layout; shuffle the cards as before, and concentrate on you. The first card is you now, the second reflects the positive things you need in your life – a type of partner, a relationship, work, lifestyle. The third card reflects the things you don't need that create conflict in your life – specific people, issues or work – while the fourth card shows how to deal with this and your options. The final card offers you direction.

sample reading

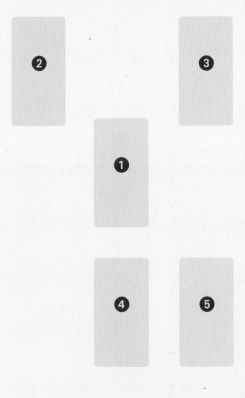

1 **The Tower.** You are going through a period of disruption. Your trust has been destroyed by unforeseen events.

2 **The Emperor.** You need a strong active, independent partner, or you need to be self-sufficient in your career.

3 **The Fool.** You don't need either a frivolous friend or lover, or to take risks.

4 **Strength.** You need courage and honesty to ask for what you want or need.

5 **Wheel of Fortune.** A chance encounter could change your life; don't ignore what is on offer.

1 **Who am I now?**
2 **What/who do I need?**
3 **What/who don't I need?**
4 **Options available?**
5 **Future direction?**

divination spread

This takes you deeper into yourself so that you can be really honest about your motivations and goals. It will allow you to question your responses.

Start by recording in your journal a personal response to each of the phrases that give meaning to each card in the layout. For example, you might answer the question 'What bugs me?' with 'my hairstyle' or 'a friend'. But that's a little simplistic; instead you might say, 'pushy, achiever types'.

Choose the five cards and lay them out face down as usual, then turn them over one by one and interpret them. Do any of the cards reveal similar responses to the answers you gave in your journal? If not, are they totally different? Whatever the case this is very revealing about your character. If the cards match your answers then it's likely you have a well-developed sense of yourself; if not, then you may need to work a little more with the Tarot as a tool for self-development. This particular example reading came from a client who was in two minds about work and love.

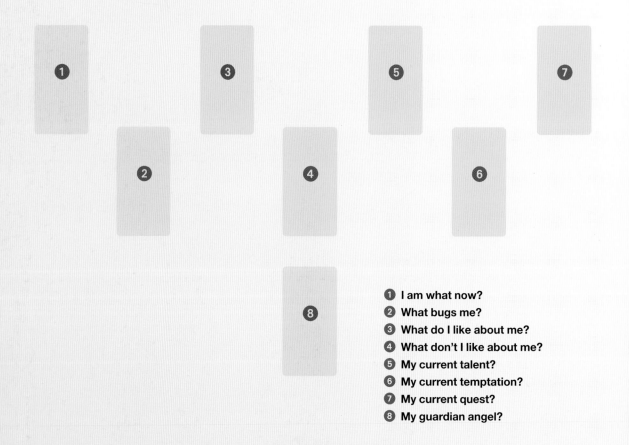

1 I am what now?
2 What bugs me?
3 What do I like about me?
4 What don't I like about me?
5 My current talent?
6 My current temptation?
7 My current quest?
8 My guardian angel?

sample reading

① **Queen of Wands.** I'm feeling upbeat, magnetic and expressive.

② **Nine of Cups.** What gets to me are smug, self-satisfied people. (Maybe that's something in myself I need to address? Do I project this on to others, and deny or repress this in myself? Do I actually come across as pushy in other people's eyes?)

③ **Ten of Swords.** I like the fact that I'm learning to accept and work with my vulnerable side.

④ **The Moon.** What I don't like is my moodiness.

⑤ **King of Pentacles.** My current talent is working hard.

⑥ **Page of Swords.** My current temptation is to give it all up for a love interest who is a lot younger than me.

⑦ **The Sun.** My current quest is to believe in myself and be in the spotlight. (That's why I'm attracted to someone who can make me feel good about myself. Do I give up the hard work and pay the price of love?)

⑧ **Ace of Swords.** My guardian angel is my ability to analyse my motives and see that I can achieve self-belief and self-worth through work, not just through a love affair.

Tracing a labyrinth with your finger is a powerful tool for meditation and can help you discover future goals.

the labyrinth

The labryinth is an ancient geometric symbol of path-walking and discovery. In this spread inspired by the labyrinth, you can explore four different paths to happiness, each based on the symbolic meaning of a cardinal direction.

North is the practical path or the path of prosperity. It is associated with the element Earth (Pentacles) and where your senses lead.
South is the path of passion and vision associated with the element Fire (Wands) where your intuition and instinct lead.
East is the path of intelligence and wisdom associated with the element Air (Swords) where the mind leads.
West is the path of Feelings and the heart with the element Water (Cups) where the Heart and soul lead.

According to ancient esoteric beliefs, each of the four cardinal points – north, south, east and west – has particular associations.

Spend some time meditating on the meaning to you of each path. For example, how would following the path of passion and vision change your life, and so on. Write down in your journal how you would practically 'walk' each path in your life.

Begin with the desire to achieve true happiness. As you shuffle the Tarot deck, see the possible paths that lie before you now and their end results. Lay out four cards face down in each of the cardinal directions (16 cards altogether) as shown in the diagram opposite. South points towards you, north points away from you, east towards your right and west towards your left. For whichever path you choose to read first, ask yourself the questions below. Then move on to your next favourite path and so on. After interpreting all four paths, you will know which is the right one for you to take.

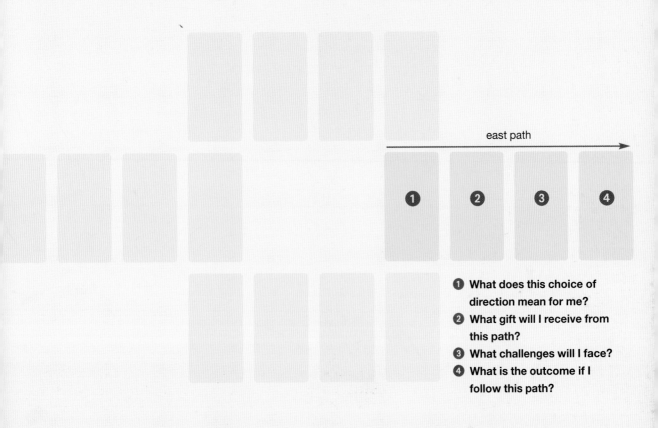

east path

1 What does this choice of
direction mean for me?
2 What gift will I receive from
this path?
3 What challenges will I face?
4 What is the outcome if I
follow this path?

sample reading for the east path of intelligence

1 **Seven of Pentacles.** If I follow the path of wisdom
and intelligence, I must be fair in all my dealings. I will
learn that in my losses I may gain, but also in my
gains I may lose.

2 **The Lovers.** I will receive a new love relationship.

3 **Ace of Swords.** I will face the challenge that I will
over-analyse everything, including this relationship,
which means my head will rule my heart. Do I then
have to choose between this relationship or going my
own way to achieve happiness?

4 **Five of Pentacles.** If I follow this path I will end up
feeling emotionally inadequate and feel that I've been
left out in the cold. Where is my heart?

the mystic seven

This spread encourages you to go deeper into the world of the Tarot and connect to the universal energy within you.

Based on the Celtic cross spread, the Mystic Seven spread adds a deeper analysis to any interpretation or question you have and, combined with numerology, offers you the key archetype that is currently working in your favour. Develop this quality within yourself and see fantastic results.

Concentrate and shuffle as before and open your mind to connect with the Universe. Lay the cards face up one by one in the order and placement shown, making sure that they are all in the upright position facing you.

sample reading for the mystic seven

In this example we have chosen to ask the question 'I am unsure of my current relationship; what is going to happen?' Unlike previous spreads we do not read the layout chronologically (see step by step below for order).

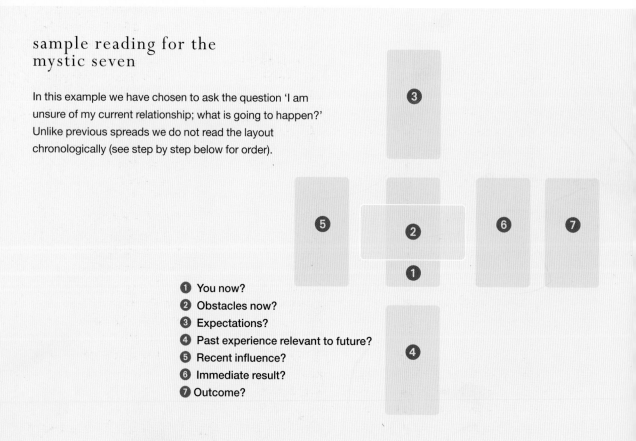

1. You now?
2. Obstacles now?
3. Expectations?
4. Past experience relevant to future?
5. Recent influence?
6. Immediate result?
7. Outcome?

❶ The first card (Justice) reveals what is going on in your life right now, your general mood or problem/question.

❷ The second card (Chariot) represents the obstacles or difficulties that concern you. This cross position holds the key to the whole question, so try to interpret the two cards together. Everything seems to be going along very easily (Justice), but your need to be in control (Chariot) is upsetting the balance. It could also be that travel or a pacy lifestyle is making the relationship more unstable than you think.

❸ Next, interpret the two 'past cards'. The fourth (past experiences) and the fifth (recent events which might need sorting out) are the Ace of Cups and Ten of Swords respectively. Once love was easy, but more recently you've been feeling everything is against you.

❹ Next, interpret the two future cards. Your aspirations, expectations and secret longings, and imminent events or influences are the Wheel of Fortune and Two of Wands. You want to take a chance now and get this relationship sorted out, and soon you'll be able to leave the past behind.

❺ The final outcome card, seven is a decision-making card defining the direction in relation to the question and where it will lead you. In this case it is Temperance. You must learn compromise and trust, and moderate your personal desires if you are to succeed in your plans.

❻ Next, add up all the numbers of each card, for example, the Ace of Cups equals one, the Ten of Wands, ten, Wheel of Fortune ten, and so on. Reduce the total amount down to one digit. So for the above example, adding the numbers:

$11+7+1+10+10+2+14 = 55$

$5+5 = 10$

$1+0 = 1$

Therefore the final number is 1.

❼ Now read the numerological symbolism for this number below, which will tell you the archetype working in your favour right now. The key to your future success lies in developing the positive aspects of this archetype in yourself with regard to this question, the numerological archetype 1, means you must express the Innovator within you to sort out this relationship.

1. The Innovator
2. The Negotiator
3. The Communicator
4. The Organizer
5. The Traveller
6. The Healer
7. The Artist/Philosopher
8. The Entrepreneur
9. The Campaigner/Crusader

mandala

Mandalas, like this one from Nepal, are mystical symbols to help you connect to the universal energy.

Mandala is a Sanskrit word meaning 'circle' and is usually a circular design symbolizing the cosmos. The mandala is a powerful meditational and creative tool for being at one with the Universe.

This Tarot spread is designed to open you to your own intuitive, psychic or spiritual powers as you truly begin to enter the 'symbolic world'. It is a great meditation tool for self-understanding, and can free you from the cares and worries of daily living. It gives you a step-by-step sense of living in the moment and connecting to the Universe.

Simply, you are going to play the part of the Fool on his quest. This spread uses 22 cards in total with the mandala symbolizing the Fool's quest through the Major Arcana, thus each placement represents the deep archetypal energy of the equivalent Major Arcana card. I've made it simple to interpret and as there is insufficient room to interpret all 22 placements, I've given you the most basic of example interpretations for a few to get you started, but I hope you will go deeper with this layout than any before.

Shuffle the whole deck as usual and cut three times, then quietly begin to deal out the cards face down from the top of the deck as shown in the spiral pattern opposite until you have placed a total of 22 cards. The last card you lay down corresponds to the Fool himself, and the key to who you are right now and the spiritual or emotional quest you must follow. But first you have to get there.

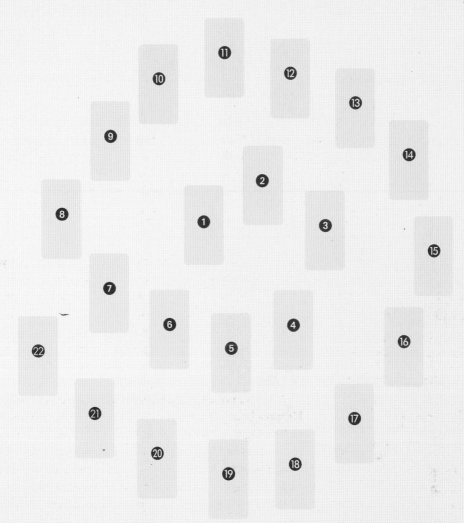

Now you can begin the journey. Turn each card face up
one by one and interpret them as the following:

❶ The Fool meets this

❷ The Fool hides this

❸ The Fool feels this

❹ The Fool ponders this

❺ The Fool conforms to this

❻ The Fool yearns for this

❼ The Fool controls this

❽ The Fool tolerates this

❾ The Fool seeks this

❿ The Fool sees this

⓫ The Fool decides this

⓬ The Fool sacrifices this

⓭ The Fool eliminates this

⓮ The Fool balances this

⓯ The Fool ignores this

⓰ The Fool adjusts to this

⓱ The Fool is inspired by this

⓲ The Fool is confused by this

⓳ The Fool is enlightened by this

⓴ The Fool is called on by this

㉑ The Fool connects to the cosmos by this

㉒ The Fool himself, the quest you must follow

sample reading for some of the mandala spread

Here are some brief example interpretations of some of the pathway. SEE that these steps along the Tarot mandala are all aspects of yourself and you are all aspects of the Tarot. BE in the moment of each step of this universal energy. And most of all enjoy the feeling of freedom, connection and universal affinity.

sample reading

① **Three of Cups.** The Fool meets happiness. Visualize your happiest moment, be in that moment. Hold it or meditate upon happiness for a while.

② **Death.** The Fool hides his fear of change. Think about whether you fear change or feel nourished by it. Imagine change as an angel who comes to lead you on to better things. Don't hide your fear.

③ **Seven of Swords.** The Fool feels a little dishonest. How honest are you with your feelings and needs? Enter into dishonesty. Imagine yourself stealing something. How does that feel?

④ **Knight of Pentacles.** The Fool ponders persistence and responsibility. What are they? How dedicated are you? Enter into the realm of 'effort without passion' in your mind. Analyse its meaning.

㉑ **The Star.** The Fool connects to the cosmos through unconditional love. Enter into the place of no conditions. Meditate upon nothingness.

㉒ **The Magician.** The key to your quest is to acknowledge your true intentions and tap into the power of the Universe to get results.

chakras

This spread is a wonderful tool for unblocking the seven main energy centres of the body, known as the chakras in Eastern spiritual traditions.

Sometimes we feel something isn't in balance and it's likely that one of our chakral areas is tense or blocked. You can't communicate to a partner properly, or every time the toast lands butter side down, you say, here we go again. What am I doing wrong? By using the tarot you can find out which chakra may be blocked and the underlying cause for the imbalance. This spread also enables you to see any psychological blockages and what needs to be expressed or worked on.

Chakra strengthening techniques can still your mind and allow you to be more intuitive and centred.

chakra cleansing

If you discover any imbalance in your chakras, do the following chakra cleansing routine:

Find a quiet place to sit or, better still, lie down. Now knowing which chakra/chakras need cleansing, place your hands with fingers touching, palms down about 7.5 cm (3 inches) above your body as if hovering above the energy. For example, in the reading here, it was the Base chakra and the Heart chakra which need attention. Gently open the chakra by visualizing the colour filling this area around and within you. Imagine this for several minutes, then close down the chakra before moving on to the next one as explained on page 43.

the chakras

1 Base or Root Chakra – your state of groundedness. Your survival instinct. Colour red.

2 Sacral Chakra – sexuality and feelings. Colour orange.

3&4 Solar Plexus Chakra – state of your ego. Colour yellow.

5 Heart Chakra – self-love and compassion. Colour green.

6&7 Throat Chakra – communication. Colour Blue.

8&9 Third Eye Chakra – insight, wisdom. Colour indigo.

10 Crown Chakra – connection to the divine, higher spiritual self. Colour violet.

sample reading

① **Knight of Wands.** Impetuous and daring, but not very reliable so unlikely to be very grounded. This chakra may need some cleansing. (See Chakra Cleansing exercise on page 123.)

② **King of Pentacles.** Sexually I'm in tune with my needs. My feelings are deep and I feel confident about myself. This chakra is fine.

③&④ **Seven of Wands, Ace of Cups.** My outer ego is very challenging but inside I do feel good about myself. This chakra is probably fine.

⑤ **Five of Swords.** I'm self-reliant and don't care much about what other people feel. I must learn to be more compassionate. This could be the real source of my problem. This chakra needs attention.

⑥&⑦ **Two of Pentacles, Queen of Swords.** I'm adaptable and easy-going, and know how to make myself clear. People respect my no-nonsense approach. This chakra is OK.

⑧&⑨ **Temperance, Page of Cups.** Harmonious energy, my insight, wisdom and philosophical energy is in a good state. No problem here.

⑩ **The World.** I have a good perspective and understanding of my spiritual values right now. This chakra is fine.

index

acknowledgements

Author acknowledgements

I would like to thank my agent, Chelsey Fox, and all the other magicians on my Tarot journey.

Executive editor Sandra Rigby
Editor Ruth Wiseall
Design manager Tokiko Morishima
Designer Joanna MacGregor
Photographer Ruth Jenkinson
Senior production controller Marián Sumega

Tarot Cards © Lo Scarabeo

Special Photography © Octopus Publishing Group
Ltd/Ruth Jenkinson

Other photography Alamy/INTERFOTO
Pressebildagentur 37; /JUPITERIMAGES/Polka Dot
51. Corbis/E.O. Hoppé 11. Getty Images/Jim
Ballard 61; /Giantstep Inc. 106. Mary Evans Picture
Library 10; /Illustrated London News Ltd. 15.
Octopus Publishing Group Limited/Paul Bricknell
55; /Frazer Cunningham 57; /Ruth Jenkinson 116,
123; /Russel Sadur 13. Shutterstock/Narcisa
Floricica Buzlea 72; /Petro Feketa 39; /J. Helgason
80; /Carly Rose Hennigan 65; /Tischenko Irina 92;
/jkitan 86; /Zsolt Nyulaszi 112; /salamanderman
33, 120; /Alexander Sysolyatin 74; /witchcraft 53.
TopFoto/Topham Picturepoint 14.